EARLY CHILDHOOD EDUCATION SERIES

Leslie R. Williams, Editor
Millie Almy, Senior Advisor

ADVISORY BOARD: Barbara T. Bowman, Harriet K. Cuffaro, Stephanie Feeney, Doris Pronin Fromberg, Celia Genishi, Dominic F. Gullo, Alice Sterling Honig, Elizabeth Jones, Gwen Morgan, David Weikart

Play and the Social Context
of Development in Early Care
and Education
BARBARA SCALES, MILLIE ALMY
AGELIKI NICOLOPOULOU &
SUSAN ERVIN-TRIPP, Eds.

The Whole Language Kindergarten
SHIRLEY RAINES
ROBERT CANADY

Good Day/Bad Day:
The Child's Experience of Child Care
LYDA BEARDSLEY

Children's Play and Learning:
Perspectives and Policy Implications
EDGAR KLUGMAN
SARA SMILANSKY

Serious Players
in the Primary Classroom:
Empowering Children Through
Active Learning Experiences
SELMA WASSERMANN

Child Advocacy for
Early Childhood Educators
BEATRICE S. FENNIMORE

Managing Quality Child Care Centers:
A Comprehensive Manual for Administrators
PAMELA BYRNE SCHILLER
PATRICIA M. DYKE

Multiple Worlds of Child Writers:
Friends Learning to Write
ANNE HAAS DYSON

Young Children Continue to Reinvent
Arithmetic—2nd Grade: Implications
of Piaget's Theory
CONSTANCE KAMII

Literacy Learning in the Early Years:
Through Children's Eyes
LINDA GIBSON

The Good Preschool Teacher:
Six Teachers Reflect on Their Lives
WILLIAM AYERS

A Child's Play Life:
An Ethnographic Study
DIANA KELLY-BYRNE

Professionalism and the Early Childhood
Practitioner
BERNARD SPODEK, OLIVIA N. SARACHO,
& DONALD L. PETERS, Eds.

Looking at Children's Play: The Bridge
from Theory to Practice
PATRICIA A. MONIGHAN-NOUROT,
BARBARA SCALES, JUDITH L. VAN HOORN,
& MILLIE ALMY

The War Play Dilemma: Balancing
Needs and Values in the
Early Childhood Classroom
NANCY CARLSSON-PAIGE &
DIANE E. LEVIN

The Piaget Handbook
for Teachers and Parents
ROSEMARY PETERSON &
VICTORIA FELTON-COLLINS

Teaching and Learning in a Diverse
World: Multicultural Education
PATRICIA G. RAMSEY

The Early Childhood Curriculum:
A Review of Current Research
CAROL SEEFELDT, Ed.

The Full-Day Kindergarten
DORIS PRONIN FROMBERG

Promoting Social and Moral
Development in Young Children
CAROLYN POPE EDWARDS

(Continued)

GOOD DAY BAD DAY

The Child's Experience of Child Care

WITHDRAWN

LYDA BEARDSLEY

Foreword by W. Norton Grubb
Afterword by Millie Almy

TEACHERS COLLEGE PRESS

Teachers College, Columbia University
New York and London

Published by Teachers College Press, 1234 Amsterdam Avenue
New York, NY 10027

Library of Congress Cataloging-in-Publication Data

Beardsley, Lyda.
    Good day/bad day: the child's experience of child care / Lyda
    Beardsley ; foreword by Norton Grubb; afterword by Millie Almy.
        p.   cm.
    Includes bibliographical references and index.
    ISBN 0-8077-3040-8 (h). — ISBN 0-8077-3039-4 (p)
    1. Child care—California—Case studies. 2. Day care centers—
    California—Activity programs—Case studies. I. Title.
HQ778.7.U6B43   1990   90-40611
362.7'12—dc20   CIP

Printed on acid-free paper

Manufactured in the United States of America

97   96   95   94   93   92   91   90   8   7   6   5   4   3   2   1

Contents

Foreword

Public interest in young children and in child care has grown enormously over the past few years. At the federal level, more than 70 bills related to early childhood programs have been introduced, and Congress is on the verge of passing legislation that would substantially expand the federal resources in early childhood programs. At least half the states now provide funds for prekindergarten programs, almost all of them enacted within the past few years, and many more states have convened commissions to consider their options. The business community has also extended its support for early childhood programs, especially for poor children. And, of course, the use of child care has increased steadily over the past two decades, particularly with continued increases in mothers working.

In this upsurge of interest, the different worlds of concern with child care remain badly divided. Policymakers, researchers, and child care advocates busy themselves with debating funding arrangements, licensing and other regulatory mechanisms, and administrative structures, but with little sense of what happens in child care settings or how the policy options they weigh affect small children. Conscientious practitioners—administrators and teachers in child care settings— worry about what constitutes good care and how they ought to respond to the myriad crises that pop up in the course of the day, but they rarely think about the policies—explicit and implicit—that shape what they do with little children, and they almost never participate in the public deliberations around public policies toward young children. Parents search for good care, limited by their incomes and by what is available within their communities, but they often are unsure what to look for and rarely understand how their choices have come to be so limited. Those who make the most important public decisions are generally cut off from the experiences of children, then, while those most familiar with what happens with young children have little voice in changing the conditions of child care.

This volume provides one way to bridge the gap between the world of policy and the world of practice. By describing a typical day in both a good child care center, epitomized by the fictitious Second Step Children's Center, and a mediocre child care center represented by the equally fictitious Wee Tots Nursery School, Lyda Beardsley provides a vivid sense of what happens to children in different kinds of settings, for those who have not spent much time in such places. By linking the experiences of children to policies about adult-child ratios, teacher qualifications, spending levels and teacher wages, she clarifies how important such policies are to the lives of children, for those who spend a great deal of time in child care centers but without much contact with the world of policy. The audience for this wonderful book should therefore be a broad cross-section of people interested in child care, including policymakers, advocates, and social science researchers; administrators and teachers interested in learning more about policy issues and in seeing how recent research can be used to improve their practice; those who train early childhood teachers, and teachers in training, who need to understand the differences between appropriate and inappropriate responses to young children; and even parents wanting to know more about what might happen during their children's day, what constitutes good quality care, and how quality is affected by various public and private decisions.

In the recent interest in early childhood programs, issues about quality have become increasingly prominent. Evidence about the positive effects of Head Start and the Perry Preschool—a high-quality, expensive program with a widely publicized benefit-cost ratio of 7:1 for its low-income children—has clarified the importance of good quality to policymakers, while parents have added their voices to the pressures for quality. Among practitioners, there has come to be an increasing consensus about what constitutes good quality in early childhood programs, codified by the National Association for the Education of Young Children. Discussions about quality often focus on simple indicators—adult-child ratios, group sizes, the training in early childhood development of child care teachers, expenditures levels, wage rates for teachers. But as Lyda Beardsley's descriptions of child care centers clarify, quality is much more subtle than these indicators can reveal. Good child care programs have very different patterns of interactions between teachers and children, and among children, compared to mediocre programs. The children in bad programs may experience rejection, defeat, boredom, and loneliness, often because caregivers fail to understand why children behave as they do and respond to children inappropriately. Conversely, in similar situations

with knowledgeable and experienced caregivers, the inevitable conflicts among children are managed smoothly and supportively, and
children are consistently encouraged in their explorations and their
learning. To be sure, large classes, the lack of appropriate training,
teacher turnover due to low wages, and the other conventional measures of low quality all exacerbate the pressures within child care
centers and make it more likely that mediocre care will take place, but
it is important to understand that these measures affect children in
many different ways, most of which parents and policymakers never
see.

By the same token, the subtle nature of good quality means that
conventional licensing, with its emphasis on crude measures of quality
and on health and safety precautions, cannot be relied upon to improve the large amount of poor and mediocre child care that now
exists. Instead, a more complex process of enhancing the training of
child care teachers, providing assistance about good practice to centers, improving the conditions (including the wages of child care
teachers) which foster better care, and promoting professional standards about early childhood programs will be necessary.

A final contribution of this volume is to insist that child care be
understood from the child's point of view. It is simply amazing how
quickly discussions of children's programs turn away from children
themselves. Policymakers and researchers examining early childhood
programs are often more concerned with reducing welfare costs, or
improving the school readiness of children who might otherwise become school failures, or preventing the pathologies that might impose
social costs when children grow up; and feminists have been concerned with child care as a way of enhancing employment opportunities for women. Early childhood professionals, who are closest to the
daily experiences of children in child care, have often been distracted
by the conflicting demands on them, the need to maintain control, the
drive to enhance the status of child care professionals and enhance
their working conditions—and have sometimes ceased looking very
carefully at children. Even the demand for programs of high quality
has been motivated less by a concern for the immediate experience of
children than by evidence about the *long-run* effects of high-quality
programs like Head Start and the Perry Preschool. But, as this volume
shows so precisely, children suffer the effects of poor care *immediately*.
For them—and for their parents, who may perceive the effects of
mediocre care without understanding their origins—the conflicts and
trade-offs that compromise quality are irrelevant. What counts is that
their experiences have been miserable, at the same time that their

more fortunate peers in centers of good quality have had wonderful times—making new friends, coming to know and love other adults who are good to them, learning many different kinds of things each day, coming home radiant and eager to return the next day.

As John Dewey once said, "What the best and wisest parent wants for his (or her) own child, that must the community want for all its children." No one wants centers like Wee Tots to persist. Replacing them with centers like Second Step will require dedication, funding, attention to children themselves—and the knowledge about the subtle interactions between child care practice and social policy that Lyda Beardsley's writing provides.

W. Norton Grubb
School of Education
University of California, Berkeley

Acknowledgments

The idea for this book emerged from my work with Norton Grubb at the University of California, Berkeley, researching a chapter on the economic, political, and regulatory issues surrounding child care in California. Norton suggested that it would be useful to provide some narrative material that graphically described different kinds of child care settings in order to illuminate for policymakers and the general public how these issues so dramatically affect the everyday lives of young children. At Norton's suggestion, I sketched out some scenes that illustrated how children's well-being is affected by the presence or absence of certain factors in their child care environments. Norton urged me to expand these sketches into a monograph that focused on child care quality from the children's perspective. He also kindly provided the support and encouragement to get that monograph and now this book written and published.

I am also indebted to the distinguished scholars and early childhood advocates and practitioners who provided insightful comments and criticism of earlier versions of the manuscript. They include Millie Almy, Sue Britson, Jim Greenman, Christine Hansel, Carollee Howes, Barbara Scales, Dorothy Stewart, Trish Stoddart, Elliot Turiel, and Marcy Whitebook.

The California Association for the Education of Young Children generously awarded me a Graduate Grant that partially supported this work.

My children, Greer and Rio, were aged 5 and 1 at the time I started this project. Two years later they are still patiently waiting for me to relinquish the computer so they "could play around with it, too." Their unflagging patience, good cheer, and affection have been enormously supportive and their continuing experiences in child care have contributed valuable material for the book. Greer's wonderful book cover design well illustrates her intimate knowledge of the subject matter.

I dedicate this book to my children, who spent ample time of their own with caregivers, mostly high quality, throughout its construction. My husband, Peter Barta, provided much of that high-quality care.

1
Introduction

"Did you have a good day?" is a question that thousands of parents pose to their preschoolers at the end of many a child care day. Most young children do their best to respond, with comments such as, "It was yukky," "I had fun," "My teacher is mean (or nice)" or, of course, the proverbial "It was okay." These responses offer clues to the child's perception of the day, but, because young children are simply not equipped to objectify their experience, they generally fail to provide the kind of qualitative information that parents seek. Astute parents may examine children's facial expressions, posture, attitude, or behaviors to get a reading on their child's day. But these methods, too, are flawed, because young children are often unable to specify why they feel or act the way they do.

"How was your day?" Not enough child care teachers have the opportunity to ask this question of the children in their care. Were more of them able to take the time to step back and consider the events of the day from the children's perspective, they might better comprehend how the physical, social, and emotional environment they have created enhances or hinders the healthy development of the children they care for. Many caregivers do care terribly about the well-being of the youngsters in their care but fail to possess the observational skills necessary to fully understand and interpret children's experiences. Further, these individuals often lack the training, and generally lack the fiscal authority, to adequately respond to the problems they do assess.

Child care policymakers and legislators rarely inquire about children's personal experience of child care. Too few of them are aware of the effects their decisions have on young children's development. Observing and listening to children describe their experiences in child care are valuable tools for familiarizing one-self with the content of the child's day. However, much goes on beneath the surface of a day in child care that may not be obvious to lay viewers and listeners but that can be revealed and inter-preted by experienced and knowledgeable observers. Govern-ment officials, lawmakers, and those responsible for developing and monitoring child care regulations play key roles in maintain-ing and improving the quality of child care in the United States. If they were to attend to early childhood specialists' explanations of how children's experiences vary as a function of child care quality, they would gain a clearer understanding of how their decisions affect children's lives, often dramatically, each day.

This book represents an attempt to consider the growing body of research on child care quality in a new light. As a consultant and researcher in early childhood education, I have found myself increasingly distressed by how infrequently educational policy or practices are informed by current research in child development and early education. With this book, I have synthesized my own observations of children in a variety of child care situations with those research findings that are vitally relevant to recognizing and promoting quality early childhood programs.

WHAT WE KNOW AND DON'T KNOW ABOUT CHILD CARE QUALITY

Over the past decade, early childhood educators and re-searchers have begun to identify a number of characteristics that most would argue are essential in providing quality out-of-home care for young children (Bredekamp, 1987; Caldwell & Hilliard, 1985; Clarke Stewart, 1982; Harms & Clifford, 1980; National Association for the Education of Young Children, 1984; Phillips, 1987; Ruopp, Travers, Glantz, & Coelen, 1979; Scarr, 1984; White-book, Howes, & Phillips, 1989).

Some researchers have focused on the relative salience of a particular aspect of care as an indicator of quality; important factors include adult-child ratio, group size, and caregiver train-ing. Usually, the quality of adult-child social or verbal behavior is the measure examined (e.g., Smith & Connolly, 1981; Howes, 1983). Others have investigated the effects of overall child care quality on specific outcomes for the children enrolled, for example, on language or social development (e.g., McCartney, 1984; McCartney, Scarr, Phillips, Grajek, & Schwarz, 1982; Vandell & Powers, 1983).

Regardless of whether quality was measured as a dependent or an independent variable, no study or review of research has yet been able to describe the conjoined or cumulative effects of specific quality indicators on the overall character of the child's experience in child care. It is one thing to say that a particular practice or set of practices has a certain effect on children's attitudes or behaviors; it is quite another to imagine ourselves as witnesses to the child's felt or understood experience of those practices.

WHAT'S REAL AND WHAT'S PRETEND

This book is designed to examine the current quality issues in child care from a child's point of view. I introduce a group of fictional preschool-age children and contrast their experiences throughout a hypothetical day in each of two very different child care situations. I describe how the children's child care experiences vary as a function of different quality indicators. Interspersed with the narrative are sections that provide detailed interpretations of the issues illustrated. These commentaries also include references to relevant research in each area discussed.

Although the characters described here are purely fictional, the incidents described are based on real observations and experiences accumulated across my more than 15 years as a teacher, director, parent, teacher trainer, researcher, and educational consultant in a variety of early childhood programs in California. I have taken real events, dialogue, and behaviors, those that I believe exemplify conditions in poor- and good-quality child care, and have reconstructed them into what I believe represents a typical day in each kind of program.*

---

*The day care centers and characters used in the two cited hypothetical examples are purely fictional; any resemblance to any actual day care center or character, living or dead, is purely coincidental.

The true anecdotes upon which these fictional children's day are based were gathered from a number of sources using several different formal and informal research techniques. Some of the stories came directly from observations of children and teachers that I had recorded during my years as a teacher of young children. As a developing teacher, I often kept detailed notes on "scenes" I had witnessed that interested or puzzled me and that I wanted to think about later or discuss with colleagues. Anecdotal data collected from my own two children's experiences in child care also generated several of the episodes that appear in this volume.

As a director of child care programs, I frequently recorded my observations of the children and their teachers as a way of monitoring and documenting the nature and quality of the centers I administered. These observations were tremendously important tools for staff development and for illuminating for parents the kind of interactions their children were involved in across the child care day. Later, as a supervisor of teacher education, I regularly used observational data as a way to inform my student teachers about my assessment of their developing teaching skills and to illuminate for them the concrete results of applying (or failing to apply) developmental theory to educational practice. Many of the incidents in this volume that serve to contrast the results of informed versus novice or ill-informed instructional decision-making come from data I collected as an administrator and as a teacher trainer.

The bulk of the real events that I have woven into these two fictional child care days came from data I gathered through my work as an early childhood consultant and researcher. Over the past few years, I have accumulated a wealth of colorful and detailed data about children's experiences in child care, generally through the use of clinical interviews, structured observations, and standardized research tools such as the *Early Childhood Environment Rating Scale* (Harms & Clifford, 1980). This research has enabled me to collect representational anecdotes about young children who are cared for in a variety of early childhood settings and whose backgrounds reflect a diversity of cultural and socioeconomic circumstances.

The two early childhood programs described here do not by any means represent an exhaustive account of all child care situations or conditions. Most notably, I have chosen to focus only on preschoolers in child care centers. Although many similarities exist, significant differences between center-based preschool care and both infant-toddler care and family day care demand separate analyses that are not attempted here.

I chose to represent child care in California, because this is where the vast bulk of my observations have been accumulated. As I will illustrate, the hypothetical California programs that I present are quite representative of child care conditions across the country. The problems of recruiting and maintaining well-trained and stable child care staff are now national issues (Whitebook et al., 1989; Willer, 1987). California's licensing requirements typify those in effect in many other states. For example, California is one of 12 states that mandate a maximum adult-child ratio of 1:12 for 4-year-olds; 18 states and the District of Columbia require a more stringent ratio (usually 1:10); 21 states allow ratios from 1:13 to 1:20 (Morgan, 1990).

I have also chosen to characterize California programs that adhere to at least the minimal child care licensing regulations imposed by this state. I do this in order to illuminate some of the potentially disastrous outcomes for children that can occur even when a child care center is in compliance with all required health and safety standards. I do not attempt to address here the multitude of even more serious issues that surround unlicensed care (unlicensed family day care and license-exempt care), which is the predominant form of out-of-home child care in California, as well as in other states (Caldwell, 1985; Grubb, 1989; Hofferth, 1989).

Many factors influence the delivery of high-quality child care. I have chosen to focus on those particular factors that I believe impact children's lives in ways that are not always easy to perceive or understand. Specifically, I examine the effects of staff training and working conditions, ratio and group size, relations with parents, curriculum, and physical environment. Although factors such as health and safety, child nutrition, and accommodations for children with emotional, social, physical, or learning disabilities are of the utmost importance in insuring children's well-being in child care, the effects of failing to meet high standards in these areas are more readily apparent and have been amply described elsewhere.

   Finally, neither of the hypothetical programs I present can begin to exemplify the myriad of possible combinations of quality factors discussed; there are much better programs than those I have invented here—and, most unfortunately, many far worse.

2
Wee Tots Nursery School and Day Care

BACKGROUND

Wee Tots Nursery School and Day Care is a large, owner-operated, profit-making child care center. The program serves 215 children in one toddler and three preschool-kindergarten classrooms. Because not all the children are enrolled full time, 132 children are in attendance at any given time. The center allows children to attend the program anywhere from 2 to 11 hours per day, 1 to 5 days per week, between the hours of 7:00 A.M. and 6:00 P.M. This flexible enrollment policy was created in order to accommodate the varying work and study needs of the parents, but without regard to the children's need for consistent and predictable schedules and routines (Clarke-Stewart, 1982; Scarr, 1984).

Ratio and Group Size

As a private child care facility, Wee Tots is required to be licensed by the State of California Department of Social Services (1986). Licensing regulations in California, as in many other states, set minimum health and safety standards but do not establish criteria for measuring or realizing child care quality as it is defined by child development and education experts (Grubb, 1989; Morgan, 1990). Because the center receives no public funds and serves a working-class population of low to moderate means, the program must cut costs wherever possible.

As a cost-reducing method, the center operates at the state licensing minimum of one teacher for every 12 children, which is reflective of staff-child ratio requirements in other states (see the Introduction). Because there are no group size requirements other than capacity

limitations based on available space, the program enrolls each preschool room up to its licensed maximum capacity of 36 children per
hour. California is one of 30 states that do not regulate group size for
preschool-age children in licensed child care centers. Twelve of the 20
states and the District of Columbia that do regulate group size require
that 4-year-olds be served in groups no larger than 20 children (Morgan, 1990).

California licensing regulations permit this 1:12 ratio for 2- to 5-
year-olds. But after a disastrous attempt to serve 2-year-olds in the
preschool program, the director set up a separate toddler program.
The toddler room operates at a more reasonable (and much more
expensive) 1:8 ratio to accommodate the very special needs (such as
toilet training) of children in their third year of life. However, experts
would find both these ratios objectionable, and for good reason.

In the past decade, early childhood education professionals and
researchers have worked together to identify standards for regulating
the quality of center-based child care programs. On the national level,
the Federal Interagency Day Care Requirements, or FIDCR, were
developed to set minimum-quality guidelines for federally funded
child care programs (Clarke-Stewart, 1982; Scarr, 1984). Because the
regulations have not yet been adopted, they are currently used as
voluntary, not mandatory, standards of quality.

A more detailed set of quality guidelines, which is intended to
serve as a standard of excellence for the field, has been defined by the
National Academy of Early Childhood Programs (National Association for the Education of Young Children, 1984). Programs that substantially comply with the academy's criteria are eligible for accreditation. In California, the state-funded child care centers are overseen by
the State Department of Education (SDE) and are regulated by a
similar set of quality requirements, contained in the California Education Code (commonly known as Title 5), which are considerably more
stringent than those required by the state licensing codes.

Both the FIDCR (Clarke-Stewart, 1982; Scarr, 1984) and California's state-funded child development programs (Grubb, 1989) require
a maximum 1:4 adult-child ratio for toddlers and a maximum 1:8 ratio
for 3- to 6-year-olds. FIDCR would allow a maximum group size of 12
for 2-year-olds and no more than 16 for preschoolers; SDE does not
currently regulate group size. The National Academy of Early Childhood Programs recommends ratios of no greater than 1:5 for 2-year-
olds and 1:9 for preschoolers in groups of no more than 10 or 18 children, respectively (National Association for the Education of Young
Children, 1984).

These recommendations are made in response to research indicating that higher ratios are related, for example, to decreased adult-child interactions and to increased adult controlling behaviors—commanding, correcting, prohibiting children (Reuter & Yunik, 1973; Ruopp et al., 1979; Smith & Connolly, 1981). Group size appears to be an equally powerful determinant of quality, with studies such as the National Day Care Study (Ruopp et al., 1979) showing, for example, that smaller groups are associated with more adult-child social interaction, more cooperative and innovative children, and greater child gains on standardized tests (see also, Clarke-Stewart, 1987b; Kontos & Fiene, 1987).

The National Child Care Staffing Study (Whitebook et al., 1989), which examined 227 child care centers in five major American metropolitan areas, found that teachers in centers that met the FIDCR provisions were "more Sensitive, less Harsh, and engaged in more Appropriate Caregiving with the children, thus suggesting that standards may contribute to the creation of a warm and caring child care environment" (p. 14). They also report a more general finding that better-quality centers are more likely to be operated on a nonprofit basis, to be accredited by the National Academy of Early Childhood programs, to be located in states with higher-quality standards, and to meet the 1980 FIDCR adult-child ratio, group size, and staff training provisions.

Staff Compensation, Working Conditions, and Stability

Staffing costs at Wee Tots comprise less than 50 percent of the program budget, which is the average allocation reported for independent for-profit centers (Whitebook et al., 1989). At Wee Tots, staff expenses are minimized wherever possible. Thus only the head teacher in each classroom is assigned a regular, full-time, salaried position. The majority of the remaining staff earn $5 per hour or less (Whitebook et al., 1989). The program employs 29 teaching staff plus 20 high school student aides. The teachers receive no employment benefits other than reduced fees for child care.

There are approximately nine different caregivers who work in each classroom per day. Because most staff work fewer than 20 hours per week and rarely during the same hours each day and because the annual staff turnover rate exceeds 50 percent, none of the children are ever quite sure who their caregiver will be at any given time. In fact, many of the children do not even know their caregivers' names, referring to them with the generic "teacher."

Wee Tots' staffing problems are not unique. A recent National Association for the Education of Young Children public policy paper (Willer, 1987) reports that recruiting and retaining qualified staff has become a serious issue threatening child care programs across the country: "For years, early childhood staff have subsidized the provision of early childhood programs by accepting compensation far below the value of their work. Many early childhood practitioners . . . receive wages below the poverty level" (p. 42). The paper goes on to report that child care is the second most underpaid profession in the country, with staff turnover rates among the highest for any industry. Others (e.g., Whitebook, Howes, Darrah, & Friedman, 1981) concur that inadequate pay, lack of benefits, and stressful working conditions all contribute to job dissatisfaction and high rates of caregiver burnout. Significant contributions to on-the-job stress include high adult-child ratios and insufficient personnel available to substitute for teachers while they are recuperating from the many illnesses indigenous to the child care environment.

The greatest body of evidence attesting to the strong relationship between staff working conditions and child care quality has been provided by the National Child Care Staffing Study (Whitebook et al., 1989). The study determined that better-quality center-based child care is clearly associated with higher staff wages, better adult work environments, lower staff turnover, better-educated and -trained staff, and lower adult-child ratios.

Staff Training

Wee Tots' teachers all meet the minimum state licensing standards necessary to be employed in this category, which are 12 college-level semester units in early childhood education or child development (at least six units are required prior to employment, with the remaining six to be earned within the subsequent three semesters) and at least 6 months work experience in a group day care program. Aides have no preservice training or experience requirement.

Because there are few academic or legislative mandates that specify the *content* of early childhood or child development courses offered throughout the state's system of accredited colleges or universities, it is possible for students to complete their required 12 units without ever becoming familiar with the special characteristics of young children's learning. Even coursework that introduces students to the findings of research in child development often fails to offer concrete methods for applying this knowledge base to their work as teachers. And because students often enroll in courses at more than one college, there is often little coherence in an individual's training and little similarity between one teacher's training and another's.

It is unlikely that any combination of 12 units of early childhood coursework, no matter how well designed, is sufficient *by itself* to prepare educators to create and maintain quality programs for young children (Almy, 1975, 1982; Bredekamp, 1987; Elkind, 1986; Ruopp et al., 1979). Many child care experts argue that *supervised* field experience with young children is of equal importance to college-level coursework in the training of early childhood teachers (Bredekamp, 1987). *Supervised* is the key word here, because research has as yet shown no clear relationship between years of child care experience alone and a variety of child outcome measures (Clarke-Stewart, 1987b; Ruopp et al., 1979; Whitebook et al., 1989).

Recent California legislation offers a promising, although far from wholly satisfactory, solution to the problem of inadequate training of caregivers in licensed programs. As is already the case in several other states (Morgan, 1990), this new regulation allows teachers in state-licensed centers to substitute a Child Development Associate (CDA) credential for the required 12 units of early childhood education. Since "certification of CDA's is based on both educational attainment and their proven competence in meeting children's needs" (Zigler, 1987, p. 258), their training would much more closely approximate the coherent program of early childhood education and supervised field-work advocated by most early childhood experts. However, the new law does not address the related concern of experts that these paraprofessionals be supervised by educators with far more extensive training and experience (Almy, 1975; 1982; National Association for the Education of Young Children, 1984; Zigler, 1987).

The recent National Child Care Staffing Study has demonstrated that the amount of formal education obtained by teachers is the strongest predictor of their ability to provide sensitive and appropriate caregiving (Whitebook et al., 1989). Nevertheless, at present, only 18 states and the District of Columbia currently require child care teachers to enroll in coursework prior to employment, and in most cases these requirements specify fewer than a total of 20 semester units (Morgan, 1990).

Curriculum and Program Structure

The structure of the Wee Tots program combines *three* distinct types of early childhood programs (Grubb, 1989) under one roof.

Because the center was originally a nursery school, the morning component of the program remains an *academically oriented preschool*. The lead teachers in the morning all have training and experience at the elementary level (usually as instructional aides) or as staff members in preschools that emphasize the acquisition of reading, writing, and arithmetic skills.

These teachers make the common error of assuming that teaching techniques that are effective for school-age children can be applied with equal success to younger children (Bredekamp, 1987; Elkind, 1986; Zigler, 1987). They believe that literacy and mathematical understanding are best taught through instruction that stresses isolated skill development. Thus the children are expected to learn to recognize letters, recite numbers, and memorize facts. Large-group, teacher-directed instruction dominates the curriculum, which is regimented into traditional elementary subject-matter areas such as math, handwriting, and art. The teacher determines and directs almost all the children's activities, which generally revolve around the use of such abstract materials as workbooks, ditto sheets, and predesigned craft projects. Children's abilities are measured by knowing the "right" answers to the teachers' questions, circling the correct items on a worksheet, and coloring within the lines.

However, child development experts have shown that young children's cognitive development is not fragmented into separate content areas. Preschoolers learn best about math, science, art, and so forth through activities that integrate concepts that are appropriately segregated into subject-matter areas only when children are much older. Young children construct their knowledge of the world through playful, self-directed manipulation of concrete objects and mutually initiated interactions with adults and other children (Elkind, 1986; Forman & Kuschner, 1983; Kamii, 1985). Developmentally appropriate practice emphasizes learning as an integrated, interactive, and self-initiated process through which children actively participate in their own education.

Child psychologist David Elkind (1986) warns that early instruction can impede children's natural motivation to learn. "When adults intrude in this self-directed learning and insist on their own learning priorities . . . a child may learn to become dependent on adult direction and not to trust his or her own initiative" (p. 635). He argues that formal instruction undermines self-esteem by making children too dependent on adult approval and social comparison for their sense of self-worth. Elkind points out that rote learning and memorization restrict opportunities for the kind of experimentation and exploration that give rise to reflective abstraction, a process in which the child not only acts on objects but notices and contemplates her own actions and that "is essential for the full realization of a child's cognitive abilities" (p. 636).

In contrast, early childhood education experts believe that teachers can best serve children's inherent desire to make sense of their world (Elkind, 1986; Piaget, 1952b) by providing them with a variety of meaningful, concrete experiences through which they can explore and test out these developing concepts (for example, talking about their ideas and adventures, drawing or dictating their own stories, counting or sorting objects that interest them, measuring ingredients for cooking). Young children will learn reading, writing, and other basic skills after they come to understand how those skills are useful to them in the context of their own experiences (Almy, 1975; Bredekamp, 1987; Forman & Kuschner, 1983; Kamii, 1985).

The early morning and afternoon program at Wee Tots reflects two other kinds of center-based care in combining *custodial day care* with *extended care* for a group of kindergarteners who walk back and forth from the local elementary school before and after school. Custodial, as opposed to developmental, care is characterized by the use of minimally trained caregivers whose focus is on ensuring that the children are kept safe, fed, and relatively clean (Grubb, 1989).

STORY

Arrival

When Jerry Spinoza arrives at Wee Tots each morning at 7:30, he likes to hang onto his mom's skirt for a while as he becomes attuned to the bustle of activity surrounding him. He slowly looks around the large room and glances out the windows that face the busy street. He bends his head back to gaze up at the familiar posters of the alphabet and of Disney characters that hang, drooping and faded, from the walls above and between the windows. Here and there, a Mickey Mouse face or a couple of letters are obscured by a colorful flyer or notice to the parents that is haphazardly tacked over them.

Even though it is now early spring, Jerry notices that the other walls are still ornamented with a long row of nearly identical red paper Santa faces, each with a cotton-ball beard and a red paper hat worn askew. These are displayed well above child eye level, in order to encourage the children to "look at but not touch!" their classmates' artwork.

His mom gives him a nudge, and Jerry runs to store his coat and daypack in one of the open wooden cubbies bolted to one of the walls. As usual, he has trouble finding an empty coathook because his cubbie is already crowded with the belongings of the three other children who share it with him.

> The cavernous building, which used to be a large church recreation hall, has been subdivided into three classrooms. To save costs, the partitions separating the rooms rise only 12 feet, not all the way to the 18-foot ceiling. Hence there is always a lot of noise, even at this early hour. Because the center policy allows the parents to sign up for a variety of different arrival and departure times, planned activities must accommodate the constant disruptions created by the perpetual comings and goings of the children.

Jerry takes a moment to lean against his cubbie, adjusting his ears and eyes to the commotion and din. Children run from one side of the room to the other, frequently bumping into the three long low tables and little chairs that fill the center of the room. One table is now covered with coloring books, used computer paper, and broken crayons. This is called the "morning art area." On the far side of the room is the stained and threadbare brown shag rug where the teachers gather the children for periodic "lessons" and group times throughout the day.

At this moment the rug is occupied by a pile of squirming boys engaged in an impromptu wrestling match. Jerry watches as a teacher rushes over to pull at arms and legs, wag a finger at sulking faces, peel each separate body away from the shrinking pile, and send them scurrying to four different corners of the room. Out of nowhere, a ball is sent flying up to the high, raftered ceiling. As it descends, Jerry shudders as he observes the same teacher, now hot on the trail of the culprit who made the mistake of "using an outdoor toy inside."

> As will continue to be true throughout the rest of the day, the teachers' primary interactions with the children consist of telling them what to do and reprimanding them for doing anything else. To a great extent, Wee Tots' emphasis on adult management of, rather than interactions with, the children can be attributed to the unwieldy ratios and group sizes maintained (Greenman, 1988; Whitebook et al., 1989).

Jerry avidly searches the crowd for friendly, familiar faces. Today he sees Gilda, the head teacher, chatting by the book corner with another grown-up. He has never been sure what her name is, so, like most of the other kids, he just calls her "teacher." Happily, he spots his pal Jamila, busily coloring at the art table, so he runs to join her. "No running, Jerry!" Gilda calls out.

"Hi, Jamila! Whatcha doin'?" asks Jerry.

"Coloring," Jamila replies and looks up with a smile. "You wanna, too?"

As Jerry eagerly pulls a chair up next to Jamila, Gilda yells out once again from across the room, "No, no, Jerry, there are already too many kids at the art table! You will have to find something else to do. You can come back later when someone leaves."

> Even though the licensed capacity of Jerry's classroom is 36 children, more than 60 different children, some part time, some full time, are enrolled in this room alone. Because of the children's irregular schedules, Jerry is never quite sure which friends he will have to play with, or for how long, on any given day.

Jerry wanders around the periphery of the room, looking for something to do. The teachers call the hours before breakfast "free choice time," which means that the children can play with anything that is within their reach. As usual, Jerry notices that his choices are limited to the same old boring set of activities and materials. He is tired of the "block corner" with its small assortment of mismatched, chipped, and dirty blocks. He has long since lost interest in the center's collection of battery-operated trucks and planes. None of them works anymore, and most of them are missing pieces. It just doesn't seem as much fun to push them around as when they were all lit up with lights and bells.

> Imagination or fantasy play is rarely encouraged here. The teachers see little value in self-initiated play and generally discourage play that is resourceful or creative, such as using the trucks' empty battery compartments to store "shipping boxes" (blocks). Jerry was once reprimanded for this activity with the advice, "Don't open that part! You could get poisoned if you got cut on the metal!" Regardless of the accuracy of Gilda's medical advice, one wonders why the staff would allow such potentially dangerous objects in the classroom.
>
> Most children are capable of discovering a myriad of interesting possibilities in even the most routine objects, but adult approval, encouragement, and even modeling is important to

validate the worthwhileness of their inventiveness. But when the use of toys is arbitrarily restricted to particular activities and not others, children's enthusiasm, initiative, and perhaps even their confidence in their own abilities can be repressed or even extinguished (Elkind, 1986; Greenman, 1988).

Jerry used to like the "doll corner," even though the pots and pans are dented, the hats soiled, and the dolls partially dismembered. But he senses that it is not "boyish" enough for him, now that he is 5 years old and will soon be a kindergartener. He looks up longingly at the open shelves along the walls where the special toys are stored, toys that children who earn gold stars get to play with. The teachers hardly ever let him play with any of them because they are new or have small parts he might lose.

Jerry rambles over to the "book corner" and selects a picture book from the metal display rack, which contains a dozen dog-eared and torn books and magazines. He flops down on the battered tweed couch and begins idly to flip through the pages of a story he's "read" many times. He closes the book in disgust when he realizes that someone has ripped out several of his favorite pages. He tosses the book onto a low shelf next to the couch where other books are stored in disarranged piles.

Many of the children's behaviors that the teachers find unacceptable are encouraged by the poor arrangement of the classroom environment. The crowded, unimaginative use of space, coupled with the paucity of supplies available for children to use independently, contributes to boredom and disruptive behavior (Greenman, 1988; Miller, 1984). The sense that children's interests and efforts really are not valued here is manifest in the use of unattractive, utilitarian furnishings, carelessly selected and thoughtlessly arranged wall decorations, and cheap, shoddy learning materials and equipment (Clarke-Stewart, 1982).

About half of the morning's enrollment of 36 children has arrived ahead of Jerry. The rest will be coming in soon. His friend Bryan and a couple of little girls whom he doesn't know very well are wandering around the room crying. They still get upset when their mommies leave. Dolores, one of his teachers, always says it's better just to leave them alone—"They'll grow up soon." Jerry does feel sort of sorry for Bryan, though, who now has his tear-streaked face pressed against the window hoping to catch a last glimpse of his departing mom. Jerry glances around to make sure that *his* mom hasn't left without telling him goodbye.

Child care experts emphasize the importance of having sufficient, familiar caregivers available at the beginning of the day to enthusiastically greet each individual child and exchange any relevant information with the parents about the child's upcoming day. For example, parents might want to note that the child did not get a good night's sleep and so might need an early nap; a teacher might want to make sure that the child brought a warm jacket that day because a walk to the park is planned, and so forth. Maintaining regular daily communication with parents, especially important during these sensitive times of transition between home and center, is essentially impossible when staffing is unstable, the group size is as large as 36, and each teacher is responsible for at least 12 different children at any given time (Clarke-Stewart, 1982; Powell, 1980; Scarr, 1984).

Although it is a common practice, it is nevertheless inadvisable for caregivers to ignore children's signs of distress during separation from their parents. Separation anxieties are not limited to infancy, can occur at any time during the early childhood years, and may manifest themselves in a variety of ways. Although ignoring such troubled behaviors may alter or repress them, it will not reduce or eliminate (and may even exacerbate) the stress that the child is experiencing. Teachers who are well trained in child development will recognize and support individual differences in preschoolers' emotional maturity and will provide appropriate comfort (Bredekamp, 1987; Elkind, 1986; Honig, 1986; McCracken, 1986; Scarr, 1984).

A Worried Parent

Annie Spinoza, Jerry's mom, crosses the room toward Gilda. Annie has been concerned lately about her son's increasing irritability and acting out. She wonders whether Jerry's behavior has to do with any problems he is having at the center or perhaps is his reaction to the thought of kindergarten, which is rapidly approaching. Just as she is about to catch Gilda's eye, a commotion erupts in the book corner, which Gilda addresses.

"I told you kids not to take any books off the bookshelves before breakfast. You may only look at the books out on the rack. Luis, if there are not enough books for you, you can either find something else to do or take a rest with your head on the table!" Then, to Annie, "Did you need something, Mrs. Spinoza? Oh, just a minute, there goes the phone!"

"That's okay," responds Annie, "maybe I'll speak to you after work."

"Well, I leave at 2:30 today and you don't get back here till 5:00 or 5:30, right?"

"Is there any other time that I can speak to you? I have some concerns about Jerry I'd really like to discuss."

"Really? I haven't noticed any problems."

"Well, he hasn't been very happy about going to school lately and he's been very cranky at home and . . ."

"Sorry, Mrs. Spinoza, I really must get the phone. I'm sure Jerry is just going through a stage or something like that."

Gilda avoids addressing Annie Spinoza's concerns for several reasons. As head teacher, Gilda is the only staff member in this Wee Tots classroom whose job description entails communicating with parents. However, she is not paid for any time "off the floor" during which to fulfill this function. Furthermore, it is nearly impossible for her to monitor the development and behavioral changes of a group of more than 60 children, not to mention finding the time to communicate her observations to each of their parents on a regular basis.

Although Gilda completed the 12 units of child care college coursework required by state licensing codes, instruction in parent communication was not specified or provided. Nor did her coursework provide her with a background in child development sufficient to enable her to interpret, or even to correctly comprehend, her observations of the children (Elkind, 1986).

Child care experts stress the importance of continuous, regular communication between parent and caregiver. Parents provide teachers with insights regarding the child's behaviors and interests at home that inform the teachers' interactions with the child at the center. Ongoing dialogue between parents and teachers ensures consistency for the child in terms of adult guidance and discipline, allows for joint monitoring of changes in the child's emotional or physical well-being, and facilitates mutual planning in support of the child's developing abilities and interests (Brazelton, 1984; Bredekamp, 1987; Powell, 1980).

The New Girl

Jerry waves and sadly watches his mom open the front door to leave the center. As Annie Spinoza passes through the door, she pauses to hold it open a moment longer to admit a woman with a little girl whom Jerry has never seen before. The girl looks scared and is holding tight to her mother's hand. The woman's eyes scan the room. She doesn't seem to know what to do. She sees Jerry and asks, "Little boy, could you tell me where the teachers are?" Jerry looks around and points at the new teacher, Ruth. He remembers her name because Ruth is his auntie's name, too.

Jerry watches as the woman and the little girl approach Ruth, who looks at them curiously. "Hello," the woman says pleasantly, "I'm Virginia Woodbury, and this is Alicia Rae. She'll be starting school at Wee Tots today." The woman looks down at her daughter with a nervous smile.

Ruth looks puzzled. "Oh, I guess Mr. Proctor, he's the director, I guess he forgot to tell us. Maybe you ought to talk to Gilda, the head teacher, she's the one with the red hair over there by the doll corner." Jerry notices that Alicia is now staring hard at Ruth's face. But Ruth doesn't look at Alicia at all; she just turns and calls out to the kids at the art table, "Put those scissors back on Gilda's desk right now, Gabriel! No one said you could do cut and paste. You're supposed to be coloring right now!"

Jerry follows Alicia and her mother as they walk across the room to where Gilda is yelling at some kids in the doll corner. "I'm telling you for the last time, Johnny, you are too big to be trying on these dress-up clothes. You're gonna get them all messed up. Anyway, you look ridiculous in that—don't you know what you're wearing is a *lady's slip*? That's underwear! Girls, what do you think of this guy, dressed up like a big sissy?"

As Gilda turns to hear the girls' giggling opinion, she notices Alicia and her mom watching in fascination. Amid the girls' snickers and catcalls, Johnny, red-faced, is ripping off the slip and flowered hat, muttering, "Well, kings dress up; I was just being a king." He throws down the clothes and runs over to a group of boys who are racing cars under the tables. He gives David a big slug in the back as greeting and sits down to join them.

Gilda turns to focus on the visitors, saying, "Some of these boys these days, I just don't know!" She grins conspiratorially at Alicia's mother, who responds by once again introducing herself and Alicia. "Oh, yes, Mrs. Woodbury, Mr. Proctor did tell me you'd be coming. I thought it was going to be next week, though. Anyway, here you are! Now, tell me, how old is Alicia?"

Mrs. Woodbury looks down smilingly at Alicia. "This lady, Gilda, is going to be your new teacher, honey. Can you tell her how old you are?"

To Jerry's surprise, Alicia pipes right up, "I three years old and I got a doggie. I gonna be learning to read soon, my mommy says, 'cause I a smart cookie!" Alicia gives Gilda a big grin, then takes a deep breath, preparing to continue, when Gilda interrupts her with a wan smile and a pat on the head.

"Well, I'd love to have a chat, but I see it's almost 8:30, time for my morning break!" Turning once again to Mrs. Woodbury, she continues, "If I don't get a cup of coffee soon, I'm just gonna drop!" As Alicia and her mom stare open-mouthed, Gilda walks away, then turns with an afterthought: "Oh, by the way, Alicia can put her things in any cubbie where there's an unmarked coathook. Also, I think it would be better if you left just as soon as possible, Mrs. Woodbury. The sooner Alicia gets used to the idea you're not staying, the easier it will be for all of us."

Mrs. Woodbury leads Alicia to the cubbies. Together, they stow her belongings inside, but Alicia keeps a tight hold on her battered stuffed lion, Jimmy, who has been her constant companion since she was a baby.

"Now you just hold on to Jimmy, darling, and I'm sure the two of you will have a wonderful day together at Wee Tots," Mrs. Woodbury says reassuringly. In compliance with Gilda's request, her mother then dutifully kneels and gives Alicia a big hug. "I have to go to work now, sweetie, but I'll be thinking about you and missing you all day." At this, Alicia bursts into tears and flings her arms tightly around her mother's neck. Mrs. Woodbury looks around desperately for some assistance, big tears filling her eyes, too.

Alicia's first day in child care is a momentous and traumatic event for both Alicia and her mother. Although Gilda realizes how difficult the separation will be for each of them, she does not feel that it is part of her responsibility to ease the process. This is partly because Gilda and the other morning teachers see their role as primarily one of providing formal preschool instruction to the children. Because their image of the learning day is modeled on educational programs devised for school-age children, they resist having to be responsible for any activities that deviate from that model. Thus they generally resent having to perform any caregiving functions, such as serving the children meals or helping them learn proper hygiene and table manners. Gilda also rightly believes that "dragging out the goodbyes" will not make Alicia feel any better; however, she has no idea how to ease Alicia's transition into the program without having her mother hang around, and she is frankly not comfortable having parents watch her work.

The morning curriculum is focused solely on promoting the child's intellectual growth without any recognition of the inter-relatedness of *all* developmental areas in young children's learning. A sound early childhood educator would recognize that Alicia will be in no position to learn anything until her emotional needs are met. Unfortunately, Gilda's narrow vision of her role as Alicia's teacher does not include the provision of the kind of caregiving attentions that Alicia so desperately needs right now (Bredekamp, 1987; Elkind, 1986; Honig, 1986; McCracken, 1986).

After her mommy leaves, Alicia lies on the floor and cries for what seems like a very long time to Jerry. He wants to walk away from her, but he remains nearby, mesmerized by her desolate weeping. Ruth comes over and tries to pull Alicia up by the arms, saying, "Come on now, dear, be a big girl, only babies cry." Alicia pulls away from her and throws herself back down on the floor. Ruth then notices Alicia's lion and picks it up.

"Is this yours?" Ruth asks, dangling the lion in front of Alicia's now-terrified gaze.

"Jimmy, Jimmy!" Alicia screams as she grabs the lion out of Ruth's hands and clutches him to her chest.

"Well, gee," Ruth mutters, "I wasn't going to steal it or anything. Listen, Alicia—that's your name, right?" Alicia nods, her chest still heaving with dry sobs. "You're gonna need to put that lion in your cubbie, 'cause if you don't, some other kid might try to snatch it. That's why we have a rule that no one is supposed to bring toys to school. Otherwise, kids would be fighting over them all the time!" At this, Alicia begins to cry again, hugging Jimmy tight and looking away from Ruth's determined face, hoping that the rule will disappear with her vision of the rulegiver. Ruth shrugs and walks away, figuring it's best just to let Alicia cry it out. As she goes, Ruth calls out over her shoulder, "That lion needs to be in your cubbie by breakfast time!"

The Wee Tots staff fail to recognize the importance that transitional objects like Alicia's lion have for children in Alicia's position. Instead of encouraging Alicia to use Jimmy as a reassuring reminder of the link between home and school, Ruth insists that Alicia relinquish her attachment to her beloved lion just when she needs him most. In so doing, Ruth not only unwittingly exaggerates the pain and stress of Alicia's integration into the program but also undermines the possibility of Alicia's forming the kind of attachment to her that could facilitate a healthy adjustment to the center (Balaban, 1985; Jalongo, 1987).

After a while, Alicia sits up, wipes her tear-stained face and runny nose on her skirt, and notices Jerry watching her. As she returns his expressionless stare, her crying abates. At 8:40, Ruth announces breakfast. Alicia, her hunger temporarily assuaging her distress, lets Jerry help her find her seat at one of the tables.

Breakfast—Conversation and Spilt Milk

"Everyone line up at the sink for hand washing and then please go to your seats for breakfast," Ruth shouts out, waving her arms to maneuver the flow of children in the proper direction. "Jerry and Jamila, pick up those crayons you were using. They're all over the floor! What a mess! I can see that Katie B. and Shawnetta and Diane will be getting a gold star for neatness today, because they hardly make any mess at all in the doll corner. Alicia, that lion needs to go in your cubbie *right now!*"

Ruth emulates Gilda's style of attempting to motivate the children through extrinsic rewards such as stickers or privileges. She rarely praises the children; instead, she issues orders and reprimands continuously.

Ruth has had no previous experience working with children, but she has completed the six units of early childhood coursework required prior to employment by the state licensing regulations. The two courses she took were "The Physical Growth of the Child" and "Creative Art Projects for Infants and Toddlers." Thus she comes to the program with neither a practical nor theoretical understanding of young children's social, emotional, or cognitive development. And yet she will now be responsible for planning and implementing curriculum for preschoolers on both a daily and long-term basis. It is hard to believe that the mere six additional units she is required to earn in the next 18 months will endow her with sufficient knowledge of child development, and its application to early childhood educational practice, to enable her to function as an effective teacher of young children.

Throughout breakfast, children continue to arrive and are briskly seated at the tables by Ruth and Dolores, the other morning teacher whose shift began at 8:30. The cook helps serve the food and sits at one of the tables while Gilda takes her coffee break. Chatty, 3½-year-old Latosha bounces into a seat next to Alicia, whom she recognizes as "a new kid" and wants to get to know.

"We gettin' cereal today," she explains to Alicia. Then, looking up at Dolores, she asks, "Teacher, we gonna get those dimestore ones, like on Muppets?"

"Latosha, I don't know what you're talking about, and, by the way, why are you sitting at this table? You go sit in your regular seat right now!"

"But I wanna sit by the new girl!" Latosha protests.

"You know the rules, now get!" Dolores claps her hands together to emphasize her order as Latosha scrambles, grumbling, into her assigned seat.

In order to maintain control over the large and ever-changing group of children in their care, the Wee Tots staff stick to a rigid, assembly-line schedule. The caregivers expect all the children, regardless of age, to remember and abide by a large number of rules and procedures that preserve these routines. These rules, such as the prohibition against choosing one's own seatmate at meals, exclude many opportunities for children to make the kinds of decisions that contribute to the development of intellectual and social skills (Bredekamp, 1987; Elkind, 1986; Forman & Kuschner 1983).

Another negative outcome of Wee Tots' poor ratio, lack of staffing continuity, and inadequately trained staff is the inability of teachers such as Dolores to accommodate to the varying linguistic abilities of the children in their charge. Dolores is unable to interpret and thus respond to Latosha's inquiry because she is unskilled in understanding 3-year-olds' speech patterns, is unfamiliar with Latosha's personal style of conversing, and is unaware of the kinds of experiences that Latosha draws on when she converses with others (Cazden, 1981b; Genishi, 1988; Tizard, 1981). It is unlikely that Latosha's facility with language will blossom in an environment that offers no opportunities for her to engage in sustained verbal interactions with adults (Phillips, Scarr, & McCartney, 1987; Tizard, 1981).

As the children begin to eat, Alicia asks if she might pour the milk.

"Well, we don't usually let kids pour the milk here, but I guess this pitcher is small enough for you to handle," remarks Ruth as she hesitatingly hands Alicia the half-empty pitcher. As Alicia pours the milk from the pitcher into the first glass, she doesn't spill a drop.

Pleased with her success, Alicia continues to pour even after the glass is
filled and looks up in horror as the milk sloshes over the sides, leaving a
big puddle in the middle of the table.

"Oh, no, NO!" shouts Ruth, wrenching the pitcher out of Alicia's
hand, "I thought you knew how to pour without making a mess!"

"Ooooo, you're dumb, Alicia! You're gonna have to clean that up
all by yourself," reprimands Tyrone, amid a chorus of snickers and
jeers from the other children.

"What is going on over there?" asks Gilda, returning from her
break. "Ruth, do you see now why we don't let these children pour?
And as for you, Alicia, spilling milk like that is very wasteful of you.
Now the children at your table won't have enough milk to drink this
morning!"

Alicia bursts into tears and runs from the table. Ruth, madly mop-
ping up the table with a sponge, looks at Jerry. "Will you go get that girl
right now and make her finish breakfast here with the rest of us!"

A number of things are problematic here. Poorly trained
caregivers often misinterpret behaviors such as Alicia's spilling
the milk as having their origins either in ignorance (or even stu-
pidity) or in deliberate naughtiness. They fail to recognize how
a child's apparent misconceptions reveal his or her developing
thoughts (Forman & Kuschner, 1983; Piaget, 1950). Without a
thorough understanding of child development, caregivers are
never sure what constitutes normal behavior at any given stage
of development or how or when to intervene when development is not progressing normally (Bredekamp, 1987; Elkind,
1986).

Instead of being sympathetic to the fact that Alicia's accident represents her understandably limited comprehension of
the principles of measurement and conservation, and thus her
ability to accommodate the difference in volume between the
cup and the pitcher, Gilda uses guilt and humiliation as a tool
for punishing Alicia's "misbehavior." In this kind of atmosphere,
the children are tacitly encouraged to ridicule and degrade one
another's behaviors whenever they appear to differ from some
expected (though often unrealistic) norm. Developmentally appropriate guidance demonstrates respect for children by encouraging positive self-esteem and by modeling behaviors that
accept and support children in *all* their efforts to learn, regardless of the "success" of any particular outcome (Bredekamp,
1987; Stone, 1978).

The problem is further compounded when Ruth delegates
her role of enforcing discipline to another child, Jerry. It would

have been far more beneficial to both children if Ruth had instead encouraged Jerry to offer sympathy and assistance to alleviate Alicia's distress (Honig, 1982, 1985). Using older or bigger children as "police" is not uncommon in centers where caregivers feel unable to adequately oversee classroom management without assistance. And although most developmentalists would agree that it is fine for young peers to remind one another of the rules, it is not appropriate for children to be assigned the role of enforcing disciplinary sanctions.

In order for social development to progress optimally, it is important that caregivers retain their roles as authority figures. Young children need to know that adults have the power to dictate and enforce standards of behavior. Then, through interpersonal relations with their peers, they will slowly begin to develop the understanding that rules are not just edicts handed down by figures in authority, but rather emerge necessarily through group consensus (Piaget, 1932). "A peer group inherently contains the dynamic interpersonal checks and balances that significantly nurture the development of a moral sense" (Segal & Segal, 1986, p. 16). Thus children need unhampered relations with peers *whom they see as equals* in order to experiment with the kind of group decision making that will eventually lead to moral autonomy (Piaget, 1932; Rogers & Ross, 1986; Segal & Segal, 1986).

Circle Time—Easter Rabbits, Alphabets, and Igloos

After breakfast, Gilda gathers all the children onto the rug for "lesson time." Meanwhile, Dolores and Ruth clean up the breakfast clutter and set up the tables for the morning projects. Gilda begins "lesson time" by taking roll.

Theoretically, Gilda can get this information from the sign-in sheet, but since parents sometimes forget to sign in and out, she rarely bothers to check it anymore, instead relying on a tedious roll-call procedure to determine just who is here on any given day. Thus begins another long morning for the children, one in which they are expected to spend the major portion of their time passively sitting, listening, and waiting (Bredekamp, 1987).

"Latosha?" Gilda begins.
"Here, teacher," Latosha responds, waving her hand so Gilda can see her behind the sea of little heads.

"Malin?" Gilda continues on through Bryan, Anthony, Jerry, Nessa, Jamila, Tyrone, Andrea, Alicia, Bradley, Jody, Luis, Bob, Benny, Yvette, Melody, Daniel K., Daniel M., David, Johnny, Rachel, Melissa, Minh, Diane, Katie B., Katie K., Shawnetta, Teddy, Gabriel, Pete, Chanelle, Jeremy, Sarah, Kyle, and Alberto, 33 of all 36 of whom are here today.

"Now we'll have singing time," Gilda announces. "Since Easter is approaching, we are going to sing some Easter songs. Let's start with 'Easter Rabbit' [traditional song, version in McLaughlin & Wood, 1969]. All together now, 'The Easter rabbit came to town, came to town, . . . hop, hop, hop.'"

Although many of the children don't know the words to the song, those who do, sing out lustily. Anthony and Benny get so carried away by the song's imagery that they stand up and begin to hop in time to the music. Gilda worries that the boys' actions, if imitated, threaten her ability to control the large group in such a confined area. She waves her hands to stop the singing and commands, "Anthony, Benny, sit down immediately! If you boys want to act like silly rabbits, you'll have to wait until outside time!"

As Benny and Anthony sit down, shame-faced, Gilda raises her arms for the singing to recommence. Soon the children are once again singing happily. Yvette is a particularly enthusiastic singer with a tendency to shout out the rhyming words at the ends of each line. Gilda disapproves and once again stops the singing to correct her.

"Yvette, you're singing too loud. That shouting is ruining the song for everyone!"

Yvette shrinks back into an embarrassed little heap and apologizes with a whispered, "I'm sorry, teacher."

Gilda begins the song again, but this time much of the gusto has gone out of the singing. Yvette, not knowing any other way to sing than in the manner she just demonstrated and for which she was so harshly reproved, sits sullenly and refrains from joining in on any of the other songs.

Gilda's insistence that the children sing in a teacher-prescribed fashion undermines the children's pleasure in expressing themselves musically. She censors Benny's and Anthony's very natural desire to accompany music with movement (McDonald, 1979). Gilda then makes the further mistake of humiliating Yvette by publicly criticizing her for failing to modulate her voice in a way that may very well require further maturation, not individual effort.

The staff's focus on acknowledging and celebrating only Christian holidays, such as Christmas and Easter, while failing to recognize the various other religious and cultural customs and events observed by the center's multicultural population, evidences subtle ethnic biases that alienate many of the children and their families and keep them from participating in the mainstream of the center's activities (Derman-Sparks & the A.B.C. Task Force, 1989; Ramsey, 1982).

After singing time, Gilda quiets the group in order to move on to lesson time. Today's lesson is about letters; Gilda begins by reading aloud from an alphabet book.

"A is for apple, alligator, and antelope," Gilda reads. "Can anyone else tell me a word that begins with an A?"

"My name has a A," responds Alicia shyly.

"Alicia, the children in this school raise their hands and wait to be called on before they speak; otherwise we would have 36 children all trying to talk at the same time. Oh, and yes, your name does begin with A. You boys in the back, can you tell me whose name begins with A? You better be paying attention now if you don't want your name on the blackboard. Luis, if you can't sit up and stop wiggling, you're going to have to take a time-out and go sit in your cubbie while we finish our lesson."

Throughout the day, the teachers rarely demonstrate an awareness of or willingness to acknowledge the special consider- ations that arise when supervising a multi-age grouping of young children. Instead, all children, regardless of their developmental readiness, are expected to participate equally in whole-group ac- tivities and to exhibit similar physical, cognitive, and social skills. Because they prepare activities that fail to adequately accommo- date the differing needs and abilities of the 3-, 4-, and 5-year- olds in their care, caregivers spend inordinate amounts of time cajoling, scolding, and belittling those whose attention wanders due to frustration or boredom (Bredekamp, 1987).

As the lesson progresses, the children get more and more restless. Gilda continually must interrupt her teaching in order to discipline those who misbehave. Dolores and Ruth sit in the back of the room and chat, periodically interrupting their discussion to bring an arriving child into the circle, or to remove a fidgety or unruly child to a solitary chair or to the even greater disgrace of marking "time-out" by sitting in one's cubbie.

Alicia, worn out from her earlier crying spell, is slowly reclining back onto the comfortable legs of Latosha and Andrea, who are seated behind her. As she closes her eyes, drifting further into a warm sleep, she is jolted awake by a sharp poke in her back.

"Teacher, Alicia is leaning on us," announces Andrea.

"Alicia, nap time is not until after lunch," Gilda points out. "If you still need a morning nap, you should be in the toddler room!" The children begin to giggle, as Alicia chokes back a new flood of tears.

Gilda may not be far wrong about Alicia, although she chooses an unnecessarily hurtful way to present her observations. Despite the fact that Alicia's verbal skills are unusually developed, she is still one of the youngest and, in many ways, one of the most immature children in the group. Because she is new to the center, the staff should at present be paying particular attention to her individual strengths, needs, and interests. These observations should form the basis of ongoing refinements to the overall curriculum plans and goals as well as informing the staff's day-to-day interactions with and expectations of Alicia, both as an individual and as a member of the group (Almy, 1975; Bredekamp, 1987).

Gilda makes no attempt to understand or accommodate Alicia's obviously stress-induced exhaustion. Once again, this is not surprising given the teachers' focus on the children's intellectual progress and corresponding unwillingness to recognize the interdependency of all areas of the children's development. Gilda firmly believes that she can best serve the children's educational needs by evaluating them normatively, expecting them all to perform essentially the same tasks, in the same ways, and to master the same unexceptional skills. To achieve these ends, Gilda believes that her teaching must address the whole group. And because the whole group is so large, young, and diverse, she spends most of her time maintaining order, enforcing rules, and redirecting children's attention to what *she* deems worthy of their interest (Bredekamp, 1987; Elkind, 1986; Honig, 1986).

After about 40 minutes, Gilda announces that it is time for projects. She has been waiting for 10:00 to arrive, when she is joined by another teacher, Alan, as Dolores leaves to help out in the toddler room. Alan is a real favorite, and many of the children jump up to greet and hug him as he enters the room.

"Jamila, Jerry, Bryan, Nessa—you children sit right back down immediately," scolds Gilda. "Alan, please join us in the circle while I describe the morning's activities." As Alan sits down cross-legged on the floor, Jamila and Jerry scramble to sit in his lap; they bump heads and an argument ensues.

"Jamila and Jerry, that's it!" Gilda shouts. "You may each go sit in your cubbies until I give you permission to join us once again."

> It is both normal and appropriate for preschoolers to seek physical proximity and affection from caregivers with whom they feel especially close. Unfortunately, these behaviors are often discouraged, particularly when the caregivers concerned are men (Richardson, 1985).

Turning back to the group, Gilda announces, "You have two projects this morning. I want everyone to do a lettering worksheet from their alphabet books. The 3-year-olds will be coloring in the letters from *A* to *D* and the 4's will be practicing writing their *A*s and *B*s. Please work neatly. I'll be checking to see that you're staying inside the lines. Then we have an art project where you will each get to make an igloo like this." She holds up a construction-paper collage. "Alan will be over by the art table if you need help, and I want you to listen carefully to my directions. First you paste this light blue half-circle onto the dark blue paper. This is the igloo, and you know it's nighttime because the dark blue paper tells you that the sky is dark. Then you make lines with white paint that go down the igloo and across the igloo like this. Then you paste a little black oval like this right here for the door."

"Can I put a chimney on my igloo, teacher," asks Jerry, "with smoke coming out?"

"I'm going to put a yellow moon on mine!" shouts Chanelle with glee.

"I don't want to make a old igloo. I want to make a sword and a shield to play Thundercats!" Jeremy proclaims.

"Yeah, yeah!" agree Nessa and Luis.

"No, no, no, children. You will each make an igloo like this, and I expect you to follow my directions carefully. Just think how happy your moms and dads will be when you bring home this pretty igloo picture for them." Gilda rises to dismiss the children. "Be sure to wait quietly in your seats until one of the teachers comes by to check your work. Oh, and when you finish your two projects you may play in the block corner or the playhouse until recess."

"What's a 'igloo'?" Alicia whispers to Nessa as they walk to the art table.

"I think it's a sorta basketball," Nessa replies.

This "art project" has, of course, nothing to do with art. By dictating both the subject and the design of the project, Gilda has successfully eliminated any opportunity for the children to exercise their creativity or express their thoughts and ideas through art. Furthermore, because the subject of the project, an igloo, bears no apparent relationship to their experience or interests, the children will carry out the activity with little enthusiasm and even some reluctance.

For children to develop a love of learning and a sense of mastery in their endeavors, it is essential that caregivers encourage the children's participation by allowing the children's ideas and interests to motivate classroom activities in all areas of the curriculum, including art (Almy, 1975; Bredekamp, 1987; Forman & Kuschner, 1983; Gottfried, 1983). This does *not* mean that adults should allow kids to do whatever they want. Rather, adults need to *set the boundaries* of the aesthetic experience by making available at all times a sufficient but limited number of art materials that children can handle independently.

The best art media are those that offer multiple, open-ended opportunities to express imagination and develop fine motor skills. Instead of monitoring children's successes at reproducing adult-made models, the caregiver's role becomes that of stimulating further exploration, discovery, and communication through art. Unfortunately, this latter job cannot be accomplished without sufficient staff to plan and supervise multiple art activities. Ideally, the children should be able to work in small groups where there is ample opportunity for independent exploration, peer interaction, and periodic one-to-one interaction with an adult (Bredekamp, 1987; Elkind, 1986; Lasky & Mukerji, 1980).

Jerry and Jamila sit side by side doing their workbook pages. "Jerry, your letters are going outside the line. Teacher won't like that."

"I don't care," replies Jerry, "I want to go to the block corner, and she never looks at them anyway. Hey, hurry and finish, she's coming."

"I should not be hearing any talking at your table, Jamila and Jerry," Gilda announces. "Everyone should be busily working. If you're having trouble, quietly raise your hand and a teacher will come to help you." Gilda circles the table and examines the children's work. "Jerry, your paper is a mess. Look how sloppy those letters are, and look at your B's—a lot of them are backwards! You're not getting any stickers today, my friend!"

Once again, a teacher reprimands a child for behaviors that result more from developmental than intentional factors. It is inappropriate to expect preschoolers, even those who are close to kindergarten age, to correctly form abstract symbols like letters and numerals. Most young children lack the requisite fine-motor coordination and eye maturation necessary to consistently reproduce workbook-perfect letters and numerals.

Alberto

When Alberto, a shy 3-year-old, finishes coloring in his worksheet, he gives it to Alan, who must check it before Alberto is allowed to go off to play. Alan is concerned that Alberto, whose parents moved to California from Colombia when he was a toddler, still appears to have little command of the English language.

"What letter is this, Alberto? Can you say it in English?" Alan asks, pointing to the hollow A that Alberto has filled in with yellow scribbles. Alberto stares at Alan, but doesn't speak. "Alberto, you need to answer me; otherwise, you can't go play." Alberto bites his lip and stares at the floor.

Ruth passes by and stops to observe. Alan tries a new tack. "Alberto, show Ruth you can say the names of these letters in English." Alberto glances at Ruth, then once more looks at the floor.

"You know, Ruth," Alan wonders aloud, "I think Alberto will never learn to speak English if his parents don't stop speaking Spanish to him all the time."

"Yeah," agrees Ruth, who also chooses to address Alberto by talking about, rather than to, him. "It's kind of a waste, really. If he can't understand us, he'll never learn anything at school."

In this exchange, Alan and Ruth demonstrate both their cultural biases and their ignorance of the process of second-language acquisition. They confuse Alberto's shyness and hesitance to speak with an inability to understand and learn in English. They believe that he will never acquire English unless his native language is suppressed. Neither teacher has the time or the observation skills necessary to see that Alberto is actually listening and learning, in his own way, all the time.

Like many poorly trained educators, Ruth and Alan fail to understand that young children are in the process of developing in all areas, including the mastery of language. Alberto needs to be encouraged to continue the process of incorporating the internal structure of his first language, Spanish, at the same time that he is acquiring skills with his second language, English. "In other words, if growth in the first language is cut off in midstream, the child may be left floundering in a new language. Research indicates that children who are secure in the development of their first language acquire a second language faster and better" (Gonzalez-Mena, 1981, p. 129).

Alberto will be motivated to learn English only when an English-language relationship is established between him and his teachers and peers, a relationship that emerges out of mutual interest and interaction. This is best accomplished in a context where new language is derived from self-directed personal experience and is thus meaningful to the child, rather than from teacher-led instruction in the sound and denotation of isolated words (Gonzalez-Mena, 1981).

Sleepy Katie

Ruth approaches the table where a group of kids are finishing their igloos. She notices that Katie K. has her head resting on the table and is idly drawing designs on her igloo paper. Katie coughs and rubs her eyes as she works. "Katie K., sit up straight in your chair and get to work on that igloo." When Katie doesn't respond, Ruth bends over to feel her forehead. "I think you have a fever; maybe we should call your mom." Katie looks up gratefully just as Gilda calls out to Ruth from across the room.

"Ruth, cook needs a lunch count right away. Please come over here and take care of this."

"Okay, Gilda," Ruth replies as she rushes across the room. "Listen, when you get a minute, check Katie K. I think she's a little sick."

As the morning progresses, Gilda periodically takes a quick glance in Katie's direction. She notes that the child does seem listless and subdued, but since it doesn't seem serious, Gilda reasons that it's easier to let her stay at school rather than taking a teacher off the floor to locate Katie's mom and make arrangements for an early pickup. Since the center has no policy regarding what, when, or how information should be communicated with parents, Gilda, Ruth, and Alan take no responsibility for informing Katie's parents about her apparent illness.

Katie's illness, and thus her inability to keep up with the day's activities, is one of many small but important events that the staff is unable to handle properly because there are simply too many children for any of them to receive individual attention as needed. Because the teachers generally focus on those children whose negative behaviors threaten to cause the most disruption, children who are sick are often attended to improperly and children who are shy, depressed, or withdrawn are often ignored.

The Block Corner

In the block corner, Jerry and Jamila begin to build a town. "Here, this is the school over here," says 3-year-old Nessa, pointing to a tumble of blocks at the side.

"Who says you could play with us?" asks Jamila. "Jerry and I are going into kindergarten and we're going to play real school and little kids don't know about that."

"But I want to play school, too," whines Nessa.

"No, you can't!" responds Jamila, giving Nessa a shove. Gilda comes rushing over and separates the girls.

"Jamila and Jerry, either you play nicely with the little kids or you'll lose your block corner privileges for the rest of the day!"

"Okay," agrees Jerry reluctantly. "Why don't you build the school bus over there, Nessa?"

"Yeah," agrees Nessa, and begins to drag chairs from the tables "to make the seats for my bus!" Alicia has been shyly watching all this from the sidelines, wanting to join in the play. Because she had little experience with peers before entering the center this week, she has no idea how to proceed to get herself involved in the game. Curious about the "bus," she moves forward to help carry one of the chairs that Nessa has dropped.

"Whoa, girls," says Alan, pulling the chairs out of Alicia's and Nessa's hands. "Chairs stay at the tables; blocks stay in the block corner." Nessa moans in protest as Alicia whispers "Sorry" and retreats back to her safe corner to continue her observations.

In order to facilitate adequate supervision of a group of children this large, the staff find it necessary to enforce a set of rules that limit the children's use of equipment and materials except in special areas and at certain times that are designated by teachers. These restrictions impinge on the children's freedom of choice and movement, which early childhood educators maintain is essential for promoting positive social and cognitive development (Bredekamp, 1987; Elkind, 1986; Forman & Kuschner, 1983). Alan's prohibition against bringing chairs into the block area serves no useful purpose other than slightly reducing the number of items that will have to be cleaned up at the end of activity time. However, his action does have the disastrous effect of repressing the children's spontaneous and creative activity, as well as once again dampening another of Alicia's attempts to engage in play with the other children.

"I know," suggests Jerry, "let's make a kindergarten room for our school."

"Okay," agrees Jamila, "which blocks do you think we should use for the desks?"

"They don't have desks in kindergarten!" shouts Jerry.

"Do, too," insists Jamila.

"Do not," says Luis, joining in the argument.

"How do *you* know, smartypants?" asks Jamila.

Before Luis can explain that he knows because he has visited the kindergarten, Gilda yells out: "All right, it's too noisy in the block corner. I think there are too many people in that area. Alicia and Nessa, why don't you go play dolls in the doll corner for awhile. Luis, you shouldn't be there at all. Alan tells me that you never finished your igloo picture."

"I did all I wanted, teacher," replies Luis.

"How will you ever get good at art if you can never finish your work?"

Once again, Gilda appeals to standards more appropriate to much older children to form her judgments about what is acceptable "productivity" for a 4-year-old. Instead of allowing Luis's interests and curiosity to motivate his learning, Gilda continually insists that he learn in the manner and at the rate she prescribes (Bredekamp, 1987; Elkind, 1986).

Jerry and Jamila decide to make a sign for the door of their kindergarten room and head over to the art table for paper and a marker.

"How do you spell *kindergarten?*" asks Jamila.

"I think it goes like this," Jerry answers as he carefully sounds out and writes *KAGrN* on the sign.

"That's spelled wrong," says Alan, leaning over the table and taking out a new sheet of paper. "Let me write it for you. Also, you used a lowercase *r* and you shouldn't mix them up like that. Here, I made you a new sign. How's that?"

"Thanks," replies Jerry sadly. As they walk back to the block corner, Jamila comforts Jerry. "Well, I think your sign was a lot better than this dumb one."

As Jamila turns to run to get tape to hang up the sign, Gilda calls out, "I hope you aren't planning to use art supplies in the block area, Jamila. That makes too much of a mess."

"I know, Jamila," says Jerry with enthusiasm, "let's take out a whole bunch of blocks and make a *whole town!*"

"Nah, I don't want to. It will be too much to clean up." Jamila sits hunched over and begins idly to stack the blocks already lying on the floor.

Until Alan and Gilda intervene in their play, Jerry and Jamila demonstrate the kind of child-directed involvement that knowledgeable early childhood educators encourage children to build upon. This open-ended interaction with objects and peers forms the essence of young children's most fruitful learning experiences.

Alan believes that he is making a positive contribution toward the children's learning by insisting on correct letter formation. He then makes matters worse when he intrudes on their play in order to demonstrate the "right way to do it" by rewriting the sign for them. By insisting that, even in their play, children adhere to adult-established concepts of correctness, Alan succeeds in nullifying the children's enthusiasm for and pride in the creative game they invented and elaborated by and for themselves (Bredekamp, 1987; Elkind, 1986).

In her efforts to ease the problems associated with supervising such a large, diverse group of children, Gilda restricts the use of certain materials to particular designated areas of the room. Combining materials from more than one area is strictly forbidden, regardless of how this activity might provide opportunities for promoting children's imagination and resourcefulness. Because the storage of materials is poorly designed, the order in the room is not easily understood or restorable by the children, who often hesitate to use materials that might require a lengthy or difficult clean-up (Bredekamp, 1987; Greenman, 1988).

Squiggles on the Window

Jerry wanders over to the window where Nessa and Alicia are making squiggles on the frosty glass. Brad, Luis, and two new boys Jerry doesn't know very well join them. Brad pushes the girls aside and beings to rub off the squiggles with his fist. "Hey, let *me!*" shouts Luis and begins a shoving match with the other boys to get a chance to rub the window before all the frost evaporates. Jerry falls backward during the scuffle and lands on top of Nessa, who lets out a loud scream. Alicia squirms past the clamoring boys and runs for the safety of the playhouse.

"Just what do you think you kids are doing?" Alan pushes through the crowd of flailing arms and legs and pulls Jerry to his feet.

"He squished me, he squished me!" moans Nessa, waving her arms in Jerry's direction.

Alan grabs Jerry by the arm and pushes him down into a nearby chair. "The rest of you boys go immediately to seats at the table and wait there until the lunch signal. Jerry, you stay in this chair and don't move until I check out what you all have been getting into."

Alan inspects the window, now streaked with water and smudgy fingerprints. "Jerry, you're almost ready for kindergarten and I catch you making a big mess on the window just like a baby. And even worse, you get into a fight over it! I'm really ashamed of you!"

"But, Alan," Jerry pleads, "I'm *just a kid!*"

Ignoring the significance and validity of Jerry's reminder, Alan retorts, "No back talk, young man! Now, I want you to get some window cleaner from under the sink and some paper towels, and I want to see this window as clean as a whistle in 5 minutes or you'll *really* be in for big trouble, mister!"

To Alan's amazement, Jerry looks up at him with a smile and skips happily over to the sink for his cleaning supplies. For Jerry, washing the window promises to be the most fun he's had all day!

Because almost all the center activities here are teacher-directed, the children spend inappropriately long periods of time with essentially nothing to do. It is extremely difficult for young children to sit passively waiting for the teacher to lead them through yet another teacher-designed and selected task (Bredekamp, 1987; Miller, 1984).

Many of the antisocial peer interactions that erupt in this setting can be illuminated in light of a recent study (Killen & Turiel, 1985) that demonstrated how the patterns of preschoolers' peer interactions vary by setting. The authors found that children's behaviors were generally less cooperative and more solicitous of adult assistance in an adult-supervised, large-group, free play setting than they were in semistructured small peer groups with minimal adult intervention. Interactions in the former setting often were marked by conflicts over adult-imposed limits and rules. In contrast, in the child-directed peer group setting, the children initiated a variety of prosocial interchanges.

The children's great interest in writing on the window exhibits not only a very natural curiosity but also a healthy demonstration of their abilities to explore materials and initiate their own modest learning project. The adult intervention needed here is not the kind that curtails the activity but the kind that supports it by helping the children redirect their competitive, antagonistic energies to cooperative interactions (Honig, 1985; Miller, 1984; Rogers & Ross, 1986; Stone, 1978).

Washing Up

At 11:50, Gilda blinks the classroom lights off and on in order to get the children's attention. "I want the boys in a line by the window and the girls in a line by the wall so we can wash our hands for lunch."

The children begin to crowd into their respective lines, accompanied by a lot of pushing and jostling for positions near the front. Jerry slides in line behind Luis and a new boy. He stares idly out the window as he waits for the line to begin to move. Bradley runs over and cuts in front of Jerry in order to be near his pal, Luis.

"Hey, you aren't supposed to butt in line. Teacher *says*," chides Jerry.

"You just shut up, fucking asshole," replies Brad with a shove that sends Jerry careening into a group of boys waiting behind him.

Jerry jumps up and grabs Brad's jacket. "Well, you're a shithead," he tells Brad, repeating a juicy phrase he heard one of the big boys use effectively yesterday afternoon.

Brad, seeing Alan approach from behind Jerry's back, decides that it would be more prudent to play innocent than to fight back. "Alan, Jerry's bothering me!" he calls out.

"What's going on here?" Alan demands.

Luis perks up. "Jerry was pushing Bradley and he even said the S-word."

"But Bradley took cuts," Jerry whimpers.

"Ooh, Jerry's a big liar," interrupts Luis. "He's always messing with other kids."

"I am not," Jerry wails. "You just shut up, you big fat buttface!" Jerry grabs Luis's face with his hand and begins to push him backwards.

Alan lunges forward to pry the boys apart. He pins the flailing, tearful Jerry against the wall, catches him by the shoulders, and shakes him until Jerry squeals, "Leave me alone, I *hate* you, Alan!"

"Well, I don't need this behavior, Jerry! Maybe now you'll know how it feels to have someone bother you," Alan angrily explains. "You go sit in your cubbie right now, and you may not get up for lunch until I say so."

Again the center's lack of adequate supervision is further compromised by the staff's choice of developmentally inappropriate management techniques. Having young children continually wait in long, boring lines during transitions from one activity to another is an unimaginative use of children's time and only invites idleness and aggressive behaviors (Bredekamp, 1987; Greenman, 1988; Miller, 1984).

It is not uncommon to hear very young children use foul language during disputes when caregivers fail to model and encourage positive uses of language to settle disagreements (Bredekamp, 1987; Rogers & Ross, 1986). Young children "easily pick up affectively important phrases without necessarily understanding them at all" (Mattick, 1981, p. 86). They are also quick to emulate the language and behaviors of older children, whom they often idolize (Cazden, 1981b). So, when children observe the attention-getting exchanges of vulgarities between their older peers, they assume that these are not only acceptable, but also desirable, ways to communicate.

Alan is guilty of acting inappropriately on the basis of several other misconceptions regarding the children in his charge. Because he has had occasion to reprimand Jerry on previous occasions, Alan assumes that Jerry is guilty of misconduct here as well. Not being familiar enough with the children's relationships, he does not realize that Luis, Brad's best pal, is not the ideal witness to report on who initiated the argument. More importantly, Alan fails to question Jerry and Brad about the source of their dispute, and he makes no effort to help them resolve the obvious tensions between them (Bredekamp, 1987).

Exasperated by the morning's constant altercations, Alan responds to Jerry's behavior as though it were a personal affront. He decides in anger that giving Jerry "a taste of his own medicine" will encourage Jerry's sympathy for others' feelings and will dissuade him from further aggressive expressions of anger and dissatisfaction. Unfortunately, Alan's demonstration of "reciprocity" only serves to heighten Jerry's awareness of Alan's role as an authority figure, while increasing his fear of the exercise of that authority. Children are not "shaken" or lectured out of their egocentrism, but rather begin to experience and act on empathetic understandings of others through observing adults and older children express empathic feelings and model sympathetic behaviors. Research suggests that adult expressions of anger are counterproductive responses to children's misbehaviors. Caregivers' expressions of real emotion—concern, disappointment, and pain—are most nurturing of the development of altruism and empathy (Crockenberg, 1985; Yarrow, Scott, & Waxler, 1973; Zahn-Waxler in Goleman, 1985).

Alicia has followed the line of girls into the bathroom and attempts to imitate the hand-washing practices she observes. She enjoys the feel of the cool water and squishy soap on her hands and rises on her tiptoes to relish a cool drink from the faucet as she rinses her hands. She lifts her head, refreshed, only to hear Melody complain, "You're a dummy, girl. See, you got your hair all wet, and now teacher is going to really be mad at you!"

"Yeah, *no playing in the water!*" Nessa scolds, wagging a finger, just as she's seen her teachers do frequently whenever a child spends "too much time at the sink."

Alicia runs out of the bathroom to find Ruth who seemed sort of nice when she was feeling Katie's forehead earlier, at least nicer than when she was mad about the milk at breakfast. Alicia hopes that Ruth won't let the children keep talking so mean to her. But when she looks around the room, she only recognizes Alan, who is busily talking to a strange new big boy and a fat lady who looks sort of familiar. Just then the door opens, and a new group of kids run squealing into the room. Neither Ruth nor that other lady who yells so much are anywhere in sight.

At noon, a small group of children who only attend the program for the traditional preschool morning hours are picked up by their parents. At the same time, a group of kindergartners arrive to "replace" them and thus replenish the 1:12 adult–child ratio that the center must maintain at all times to support itself. Also at the same time, Gilda leaves for her lunch hour and is replaced by Dolores, who returns to the preschool room for half an hour before her daily shift ends. Ruth's 4½-hour day ends, and she is replaced by Billy, the cook's 18-year-old assistant, who has been subbing in this position for the last week because no qualified teacher or substitute teacher has been found to fill the vacant afternoon floating teacher's slot. (The "floating teacher" works for an hour or so in each classroom to cover teacher breaks and then finishes the day in the toddler room.) This practice of using unqualified, nonteaching personnel as temporary substitutes is specifically allowed in the licensing regulations.

"How was Katie's morning?" inquires her mom as she passes Dolores on the way in the door. "She didn't sleep well last night, and I was worried she might be coming down with something."

"Oh, she's been fine," Dolores replies, completely ignorant of the fact that Gilda and Ruth had noticed signs that Katie was feverish and ill earlier that morning. "I think she really enjoyed the art project. They made igloos this morning!"

At this moment, there is no staff person on the floor who has been with the children throughout the morning and who can respond knowingly to the exiting preschoolers' parents inquiries about their children's day. Not all the parents realize this, however. Some choose to monitor their children's activities by consulting with staff members who do their best to reconstruct the child's day, though often without admitting to the speculative nature of their accounts.

Lunchtime

As other parents file into the room, looking for their kids, Alicia runs to the door, anxiously looking out for her mom. She walks out on to the porch to get a better look and is quickly hauled back into the room by Billy, who barks, "Hey, get back in here! What do you think you're doing?"

Alicia screams and struggles out of Billy's grasp. She runs across the room toward Alan shrieking, "My mommy, I want my mommy *now!*"

Billy calls out to Alan, "What's this girl's problem? Is she new or something?"

"Yeah, lemme check when she's supposed to go home," Alan replies as he peels Alicia's clinging hands from around his knees. "What's your name again?" he asks as he leafs through the sign-in sheet to determine her scheduled pickup time.

"Alicia Rae," she replies, her chest heaving with big sobs.

Dolores strolls over and motions Billy to supervise the tables of hungry kids, now squirming in their seats, anxiously awaiting the arrival of lunch. "I know this girl; she's new. I was here when her mom dropped her off this morning." She kneels and beckons gently to Alicia. "Come here, hon, your mommy won't be here until after nap today, but why don't you come with me and we'll set you down for a nice lunch." Alicia looks gratefully into Dolores's kinds eyes and follows her obediently to the table. "Now you sit right here, and lunch will be along in a minute."

As Dolores moves across the room to help the newly arriving kindergartners settle down at their table, Alicia jumps up and grabs Dolores's hand. "Stay; lunch with me," she pleads. Dolores sighs, looks sympathetically down at Alicia, and calls out to Alan, "I'll take this table today, Alan. Can you handle those wiggle worms over at the big kid table?"

"Sure, Dolores, but you better not spoil that girl into thinking she can always get you to do what she wants."

Dolores returns to supervise the table at which Alicia is seated. For the first time today, Alicia begins to relax, comforted by the belief that she has finally found a friend. She doesn't even mind when some of the girls begin to tease her about spilling the milk at breakfast, because Dolores isn't mad at her about that. After the meal, the children are instructed to scrape their plates into a large garbage bin and then to put their dishes into a dish-washing tray. Alicia walks ever so carefully over to the bin, determined not to spill another thing today.

As Alicia gingerly scrapes her rice and chicken bones into the garbage, she notices Dolores putting on her coat and heading for the door. "No, no!" Alicia wails, letting her fork and plate fall into the bin and racing over to hang onto Dolores's purse.

"Oh, Alicia, I have to go home now; my work is all done for today. And thank goodness, too," she adds with a wink at Alan.

"Mommy, mommy, I want my mommy!" Alicia falls to the floor, weeping.

"Well, I'm sorry, but I do have to go. You'll feel better after you have a good nap." Dolores gives Alicia's head a final pat as she scurries out the door.

Alicia continues to lie on the floor, sobbing into her folded arms. Alan lifts her to her feet and says, "You need to go get your dishes out of the garbage bin right now, Alicia. Then you can line up with the other kids by the door for recess time." Alicia drags her feet, whimpering, as she returns to the garbage can. The other children move back, excited to see how Alicia will react to having to put her hand down into the slimy abyss.

"Ooh, it's yukky, girl," cautions Andrea with a giggle.

"My mommy says you can get a bad disease from touching garbage," adds Jamila with a worried look. Alicia gasps and draws back her hand. She looks appealingly at Alan.

"We have rules at this center, Alicia, and you'll have to learn to follow them like all the other kids. Please fish out your plate and fork right this minute!" Alan demands with a scowl. Amid the snickers and jeers of her classmates, Alicia wordlessly complies.

Just as Alicia takes the first steps toward developing a trusting relationship with Dolores, an adult whom she identifies as offering her real sympathy and protection, Dolores's shift ends and Alicia is once again "abandoned" to the company of unfamiliar adults and hostile peers. Because of their unstable work schedules, abbreviated work hours, poor compensation, and generally difficult working conditions, most of the staff are unable or reluctant to form more than superficial relationships with any of the children or their parents (Whitebook et al., 1989). Like overworked nurses in nursing homes, many of these teachers believe it is better for all concerned that they refrain from "getting involved with" their charges. Rather, they choose to remain aloof, insisting on universal adherence to a set of rules that are intended to minimize chaos but that also severely limit the exercise of individual skills, interests, or needs (Brede-kamp, 1987).

These incidents illustrate some of the multiple problems associated with high staff turnover, irregularity in assigned work hours and responsibilities, and the use of interchangeable caregivers. Many early childhood educators assert that a central feature of a successful child care placement is the opportunity for the child to form an attachment to one primary caregiver who is actively involved with and continually available to the child throughout the bulk of the child care day. For parents, too, the opportunity to participate in an ongoing dialogue with their child's "special teacher" ensures an optimal continuity between the often fragmented worlds of family life and child care (Cazden, 1981b; Clarke-Stewart, 1982; Clarke-Stewart & Gruber, 1984; Cummings, 1980; Howes, 1987; Kilmer, 1980; Powell, 1980; Tizard, 1981).

Outside Time

After lunch is "yard time," and Jerry waits impatiently by the door for the rest of the class to line up behind him.

"This door will not be opened until everyone is lined up quietly and neatly," warns Alan. "We may have to wait here until yard time is over if some of you don't quiet down. This means you, Jody and Melissa. Anthony, I saw you shoving. Get to the back of the line!"

Waiting in line makes Alicia feel sleepier than ever. She opens her mouth to let out a big yawn, then slaps her hand across her face, remembering Mommy's order that you must always cover your mouth when you cough or yawn. Then sadness wells up inside her, she misses Mommy so. Tears push out from behind her eyes, but she rubs them away and looks at the ground when she sees that the big boy is staring at her with a mean look on his face. "Are you gonna start crying *again*?" Billy asks with a sneer.

"No," mutters Alicia and bites her lip.

Finally, the doors are opened and the children fly out of the room, hooting and leaping with the joy of movement. Jerry heads straight for the swings and manages to capture one before the faster-footed kindergartners descend. He begins to pump himself as high as he can go, soon soaring over the heads of the many children aimlessly milling around the yard, waiting for an opportunity to use what little play equipment exists.

Licensing codes mandate that the outdoor space (at least 75 square feet per child) and outdoor equipment provided must be "free of hazards"; however, no regulations govern the amount or nature of the equipment available. Therefore, the Wee Tots administration decided to eliminate all but one of its sandboxes because they were too messy and required constant maintenance to keep them "free of hazardous foreign materials" as required. Now the children dig with sticks in the little dirt islands surrounding the few trees that dot the asphalt yard. Rising liability insurance costs also threaten the removal of the swings and slide because the program can no longer afford the costs for upkeep and for sufficient supervisory personnel to ensure that the children use the equipment safely.

Grass and shrubbery were also eliminated in an effort to further reduce maintenance costs. Over the years, what had been a tree-shaded, rolling lawn has gradually been cleared and flattened into a hygienic but barren parking lot of a playspace. What little play equipment remains consists mainly of a steel climbing structure bolted to the ground, the aforementioned swings (at least half of which are always in a state of disrepair), a few battered tricycles and other worn-out riding toys that the children are allowed to "sign up" for, and an assortment of poorly inflated balls whose number decreases almost daily as they "disappear" over the fence into the flow of busy traffic, whose noise and emissions further pollute the litter-strewn yard.

Child care environmental expert Jim Greenman (1988) warns that when programs eliminate opportunities for children to use their bodies and equipment in ways that involve minor risks and messiness, unwanted consequences may result. In the absence of physical challenge, children may become bored and withdrawn or aggressive, seeking stimulation from peers through hitting, pushing, or kicking. "Or challenge is found illegally: climbing on shelves, escaping to other rooms, knocking about to get a reaction. The net effect is often that the potential for harm is not reduced, only the source of harm is redirected" (p. 77). It is likely that, instead of repressing their desire for physical experimentation, children will defer it to a time or situation that might be truly dangerous.

"Teacher, Jerry's been swinging a really long time," Bradley addresses any adult within hearing distance. "And I've been waiting for a turn since yesterday."

Billy has been lying on a bench, arms over his face, soaking up the sun. When he hears Bradley's plea, he calls out, without moving, "Jerry, you get ten more swings, then it's this kid's turn."

"That isn't fair, I just got on," moans Jerry, his brief reverie interrupted.

Billy begins to count, "One, two, three . . ."

"I hate this!" Jerry shouts in anger, leaping off in midswing.

Once again, a caregiver intervenes to prescribe a method for settling a dispute. Neither Jerry nor Bradley is encouraged to negotiate their mutual desire to use the swing. Instead, Jerry is expected to adhere to Billy's arbitrary mandate, which not only cuts off his turn prematurely but also violates his enjoyment of what little time he has left to enjoy his swing. Notice that neither of the boys even attempts to address the other; they have become accustomed to depending on adults to referee their disagreements (Bredekamp, 1987; Killen & Turiel, 1985).

Jerry joins Chanelle and Bob, who are leaning with their faces pressed up against the chain-link fence that faces the busy street.

"What are you guys doing?" Jerry asks.

"We're lookin' at the park," Bob replies.

"Yeah," adds Chanelle, "you just smash your face up to the fence and then you turn your head just like this and then you can see the park down the street there. Look, see that kid climbing on that big boat!"

Jerry accepts Chanelle's suggestion and presses his face against the fence so he, too, can get a glimpse of the edge of the inviting city park that is just a little over a block away.

"Yeah, that boat's neat; my mom takes me there sometimes on the way home," Jerry explains.

"You're lucky," responds Bob sadly, "I never got to go there. I wish we could go right now, don't you?" he adds wistfully.

Even though the park is a short walk away, the teachers don't feel comfortable taking the children across the busy street and supervising them in the large, unfenced park; they simply lack sufficient personnel to ensure that even such a modest field trip would be safe and uneventful. Although state licensing allows a 1:12 ratio for field trips, the regulations go on to point out that "activities outside the perimeter of the licensed day care center pose additional hazards to children. An effort should be made to gain an adult-child ratio of at least 1:6 through the use of adult volunteers" (State of California Department of Social Services, 1986, Section 101316.5, a.2). Wee Tots' owner-operator, Mr. Proctor, has been unsuccessful in attracting reliable volunteers and is concerned about the potential liability risks such poorly supervised trips would incur; thus he has decided to eliminate even the most innocuous of field trips from the curriculum.

Jerry runs to the center of the yard, where some boys are throwing balls around. Soon an informal game of dodgeball develops. The girls who are playing nearby are quietly designated as targets. Jamila, Rachel, Jody, and even little Nessa run squealing and giggling as the balls come whizzing past them. Alicia, stooping to dig beneath one of the trees, falls over screaming as a ball bounces sharply off the back of her head. The yard-duty teachers pause reluctantly in the midst of an absorbing conversation to search for the origin of the screams. "Oh, it's that damn new girl, Alicia," mutters Alan, peeling himself away from the group. "I told Gilda I thought she was too young for this program. She's been causing problems all day."

Because the staff view time outdoors as an opportunity for the children to use up excess energy, no organized activities are planned. Instead, the teachers use this time to huddle together for a chat. They leave their adult company only long enough to quell the numerous disturbances that arise when children are bored or spend long periods of time waiting for something to play with, or to attend to the victims, like Alicia, of the many "accidents" that occur when children are left essentially unsupervised (Bredekamp, 1987; Greenman, 1988; Miller, 1984).

Outdoor time is an integral part of any sound early childhood curriculum. But when adults fail to adequately supervise, organize, or interact with young children during group games or other outside activities, rich opportunities for promoting social development are lost. Without sufficient or appropriate equipment, the children are also denied the chance to practice large muscle skills. And without thoughtfully planned outdoor experiences, the children also miss out on opportunities to learn about their environment (for example, comparing fallen leaves, planting a garden, and observing insect life) (Bredekamp, 1987; Forman & Kuschner, 1983; Kamii & DeVries, 1980).

Naptime

At 1:00, Gilda stands on the porch and blows a shrill whistle for attention. "I want all my preschoolers to *quietly* line up at the door for naptime." As the children slowly begin to form two raggedy lines, Gilda continues. "Please remember to wash your hands and fold your clothes neatly in your cubbies before you get on your mats. Don't forget to use the toilets *now* if you need to. There will be no getting up until nap is over."

As Jerry, Benny, Tyrone, Bryan, Luis, Bradley, Anthony, Bob, Daniel M., David, Johnny, Alberto, Minh, Latosha, Malin, Alicia, Melody, Nessa, Jamila, Jody, Melissa, Rachel, Chanelle, and Andrea file into the room, leaving the kindergartners—Carlos, Dorette, Shane, Latrina, Seth, and Nelson—to play on in the yard, they hear the teachers from the other preschool rooms make similar announcements from their porches.

After lunch, Wee Tots' program structure changes as the nursery school part of the day (i.e., the "educational" component) ends and the day care (i.e., custodial care) begins. At 1:00 P.M., another small group of preschoolers leaves, bringing the group size down to 30, including the six kindergarteners. The center is then able to replace the third teacher position with two aides and still maintain the required ratio of one teacher and one aide for every 15 children in attendance.

Although more adults are present in the afternoon, they form an even less coherent and experienced team than do the morning staff. Because the afternoon teachers see themselves as essentially supervisors of the children's rest and recreation, they do little planning or organizing of activities. Beyond imposing endless disciplinary actions, the afternoon caregivers only infrequently engage in conversation or initiate any other positive interactions with the children.

The program's lack of emphasis on adult-child verbal exchange is particularly unfortunate. Research has shown that children's language development profits from communication with adult caregivers, especially those who listen and adapt their conversational style to correspond with the individual child's. The subject matter of the verbal interactions between children and their teachers is also important. Conversations that involve the giving and requesting of information provide valuable experience toward developing children's language skills. This is not the case in situations where children are expected to listen passively and respond silently to adult commands or directives (McCartney, 1984). Other researchers emphasize the importance of small groups and stable, consistent adult-child relationships that together seem to promote "informative," response-provoking remarks rather than "managerial" talk (Cazden, 1981b; Tizard, Cooperman, Joseph, & Tizard, 1972).

Alicia blinks her eyes as she enters the darkened room. The windows are now masked by heavy curtains, the tables and chairs are stacked in the back of the room, and brown mats have mysteriously appeared all over the floor. Everyone is suddenly so quiet, and she begins to get afraid. She watches the children wordlessly removing their pants and shoes and putting them in their cubbies. She decides she better do the same, but she can't get her shoelaces undone. As she struggles, she looks up to see Gilda looming above her. "Someone should tell your mother to get you shoes with VELCRO® ties, young lady," Gilda mutters as she pulls the shoes from Alicia's feet. Once again, the word *mother* brings a flood of tears to Alicia's eyes. She *really* wants Mommy now.

Alicia glances back longingly at Jimmy, stuffed under her jacket in her cubbie, and then silently follows Gilda across the darkened room. Gilda motions her to lie on a mat next to the bookshelf and hands her a small, thin blanket. Not feeling cold, Alicia decides to fold up the blanket to use as a pillow. She feels pretty good about her little "invention" until Malin whispers from the next mat, "You can't do that to your blanket. It's against the rules." Alicia lies there, staring at the ceiling as the rest of the children find their mats and lie down. She decides that looking at a book might be fun, but as she reaches for the bookshelf, the lights go out and the room becomes almost black. Alicia throws the blanket over her head and huddles in a frightened ball.

From somewhere near the middle of the room, a little light appears. "There goes Gilda with that dumb flashlight," whispers Jerry. Jamila and Daniel M. let out nervous giggles in reply.

"SSSSSHHHHHH!" Gilda hisses. "I want absolute quiet and that means you, Jerry!"

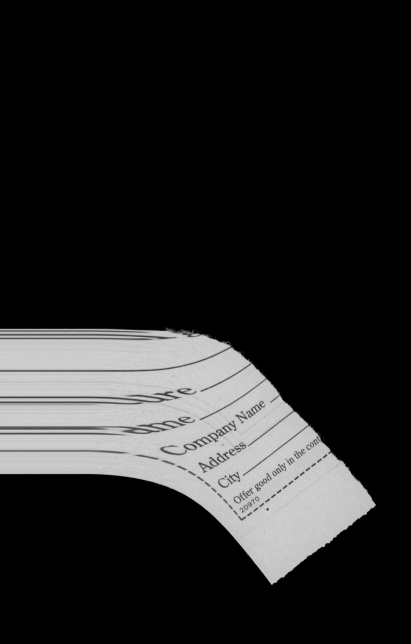

Jerry sighs and lies back down to prepare himself to suffer through another tedious naptime. He stares at the ceiling and listens to the muffled sounds of whispers and giggles coming over the wall from the other classrooms. Some of the toddlers are crying, and he hears the teachers trying to hush them. He hates that sound and stuffs his fists into his ears trying to drown out the quiet noise. Because he never falls asleep anymore, Jerry will spend the next hour and a half tossing and turning, biting his fingernails, and pulling apart his blanket, thread by thread.

Licensing regulations allow the teacher-child ratio to rise to 1:24 during napping period. Wee Tots takes full advantage of this by assigning one teacher to each room of 24 napping children. The remaining staff is assigned to either supervise the kindergartners, who continue to play outside, set up the afternoon snack, or complete clerical or maintenance tasks. Because the program provides no compensation for teacher preparation time, Gilda uses this time for planning her morning lessons.

Gilda believes that the flashlight enables her to read and write without disturbing the children's sleep. In actual fact, there is no need for the room to be completely without illumination, for truly sleepy children will sleep, probably even more comfortably, in a semidarkened room. Gilda has found, however, that the only way to manage the "resters" like Jerry is to keep them in complete darkness. She feels sure that allowing them to pursue even quiet activities such as looking at books would require additional supervision, and she needs this time to prepare her curriculum.

Instead of requiring all children universally to submit to an adult-imposed 2-hour midday rest, child developmentalists suggest that all-day programs provide an adequate alternation of quiet and active times *throughout* the program day. Alicia's exhaustion early in the day could have been ameliorated by caregiver practices that support a younger child's need for a balance between carefully planned small-group, quiet-down activities and periods of intense activity. Because most, but not all, preschoolers as well as many kindergartners need daily naps, naptime should be an option that is encouraged for children based on individual assessment of a child's need for actual sleep. For those, such as Jerry, for whom a rest, rather than sleep, is the desirable option, alternate quiet activities should be provided (Bredekamp, 1987).

At 2:30, Gilda leaves and is quietly replaced by Mrs. Howard, the afternoon head teacher. Mrs. Howard opens the curtains enough to

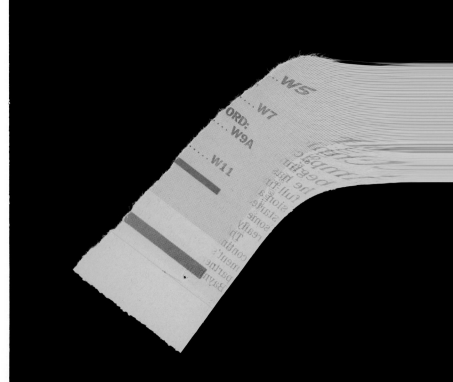

allow in sufficient light to see just who is sleeping and who isn't. She silently motions to the children who are awake and allows them to tiptoe, one by one, to their cubbies to begin to dress. Jerry is especially quiet because he knows that anyone who fools around will be sent back to his or her mat. He looks up gratefully at Mrs. Howard, who is placing a small pile of books on the rug in front of the uncurtained window for the "early risers" to look at until naptime officially ends.

Afternoon Exercise—The Purse

At 3:00, Mrs. Howard turns on lights and throws open the rest of the curtains. Rosa and Marti, the teenage aides, enter with the kindergartners, who are hot and breathless from their long period of outdoor play. Suzanne, the young college student who is the other afternoon teacher, arrives and kneels on the rug to rouse the late sleepers. Alicia, who has only just recently fallen into a deep and troubled sleep, feels herself being shaken. She opens her eyes in fright as she sees Suzanne's unfamiliar face hovering over her. She looks around in wonder, finding that she doesn't recognize any of the adults who now bustle around the room, piling up the mats and moving back the tables and chairs.

The noise level in the room increases steadily as the children race around, getting dressed and shaking out their now-rested muscles. In contrast, the kindergartners move listlessly to their seats at the tables, where several of them attempt to rest their weary heads. "Sit up with your hands in your laps, children," advises Mrs. Howard. "When everyone is seated and quiet, we can have our snacks."

After snacks, the preschoolers are shooed out to the yard for more "exercise." Mrs. Howard stays in the room with the kindergartners, most of whom are now lying on the rug, looking at books. Since th children are quiet and occupied, Mrs. Howard uses this time to se the afternoon activities. She hates to have any kind of mess to clean at the end of the day, so she tries to find activities that will maintain the children's interest without allowing them to make a mess. For this reason, the block area and any art supplies other than crayons and markers are off-limits in the afternoon. She begins to put simple puzzles, coloring books, and board games out on the tables. Just then, Suzanne enters with Bradley, who is writhing in pain over a badly skinned knee.

"I'm going to have to get this washed off and bandaged," says Suzanne apologetically. "Would you mind keeping an eye on the kids outside, Mrs. Howard? Marti is in the office making a phone call to her boyfriend, and I'm not so sure that girl Rosa's really in control."

Mrs. Howard sighs and lifts herself heavily from the chair. "Now, while I'm outside I don't want any shenanigans from you," she announces with a stern look at the kindergartners.

As Mrs. Howard enters the sunlit yard, Rosa is nowhere to be seen and chaos has erupted already. Betty, the toddler teacher, comes hurrying over to complain. "Some of those boys of yours insist on going down the slide backward, although I've told them repeatedly to stop. I've got my hands full already with these little ones today and two totally incompetent subs. I can't be responsible for your wild ones, too."

"But where is Rosa? Suzanne left her in charge." Just then, Mrs. Howard feels a tug at her skirt. She looks down to see little Melody, obviously quite agitated. "Can you just wait on this, honey? I'm trying to find Rosa. If someone's been messing with you, just tell them I'll be there to deal with them in a minute!"

"But it *is* Rosa, teacher. She's been yelling at all the kids, and she pulled Jerry's arm real hard. She's over there now, behind the bike shed."

Melody grabs Mrs. Howard's hand, and together they approach the bike shed. As they turn the corner, they hear Rosa's shrill adolescent voice shaking with anger. "You stupid little shit, I'm gonna tell Mr. Proctor what you did, and he's *never* gonna let your mama bring you here again!" They turn the corner to find Rosa, teeth bared, hair flying, brutally shaking Alicia by the shoulders as she screams into her face. Alicia is sobbing, nearly hysterical with fear.

Mrs. Howard wrenches Alicia out of Rosa's grasp. She cradles the wailing child in her arms, sits down cross-legged with her on the ground, and begins to rock and soothe her. As Alicia's sobs begin to subside, Mrs. Howard glares at Rosa. "What could this child have possibly done to make you talk to her like that?" As she waits for a response, she looks past Rosa to see a dazed Jerry, sprawled on the ground amid a scattered assortment of objects, including a broken bottle of nail polish, an overturned purse, and several dozen pencils and markers. "Now who brought those pencils outside? Did you, Jerry?"

"No, teacher, we just found them in this old purse. We didn't know it belonged to anybody. We just found it in the shed and . . ."

"He's lying, Mrs. Howard," Rosa interrupts. "They took them from the room, and I was just trying to get them back."

"Can you tell me what happened, Alicia? It *is* Alicia, right?" Mrs. Howard pauses in her rocking to look into the little girl's tear-filled eyes.

Alicia takes a shuddery breath and answers. "That boy, Jerry, teacher, he said I could play with that pretty bottle, but I didn't mean to broke it, honest!" Alicia collapses into tears.

"Jerry didn't steal those pencils, teacher," Melody pipes up. "We saw them fall out when he shook the purse upside down. Didn't we, Latosha?" Latosha comes forward, enthusiastically nodding her head.

"Rosa, I want you to go to the room with the kindergartners," Mrs. Howard directs in a somber tone. "We'll talk about this after school." Rosa sullenly gathers her things back into her purse, leaving the pencils and markers still scattered on the ground.

"I'll pick them up, teacher!" Melody volunteers. As she scrambles for the pencils, she is joined by several of the other children who have been watching this entire episode in bug-eyed fascination.

Mrs. Howard lifts Alicia off her lap and rises to her feet with a grunt. Just then, Betty comes racing around the side of the shed with a frantic look. "Mrs. Howard, *please*, your kids are fighting now, and you've got another one with a skinned knee!"

Mrs. Howard ambles back out to the yard, leaving the whimpering Alicia and the still-dazed Jerry, now rubbing his bruised arm, to fend for themselves. Melody, Latosha, Anthony, Bob, and Benny skip giggling back into the sunlight, clutching the now-battered pencils and markers to their chests.

Rosa is one of the group of teenage students who work in pairs as afternoon aides at Wee Tots as part of an occupational-training program sponsored by their high school. Licensing regulations permit the use of aides under 18 years of age in these circumstances. Each student is expected to work 4 hours per day twice a week. On school holidays, the center always has a difficult time finding subs to replace the vacationing students.

Because the students are only paid a token stipend, even less than the minimum wage paid to the other junior staff members, Wee Tots is able to reduce its daily personnel costs substantially. There is an important trade-off, however, in terms of the quality and stability of care that these young people are able to provide, to which Rosa's poor behavior attests. However, to some degree Rosa's anger is understandable, since she is expected to perform all the duties of a regular staff person but does not have the benefits of comparable training or compensation.

At age 16, Rosa is clearly not mature enough to be left in charge of a large group of young children. The children soon discover her vulnerability and exploit her lack of authority by refusing to comply with her inept attempts to discipline them. In frustration, Rosa relinquishes what little authority she possesses and defends herself as another child might—with insults, threats, and physical retaliation. Without the continual direct supervision of a competent mentor teacher, no inexperienced aide can be expected to gain the kind of knowledge and self-confidence that is essential to commanding young children's respect (Bredekamp, 1987).

Late Afternoon Activities—Waiting Games

At 4:30, Mrs. Howard comes out to the porch and blows the whistle. "Time to come in and wash up for end of the day activities! I want to see two neat lines out here right away. Chanelle, look how dirty you got your pretty dress; your mama is going to have a fit, girl! Alberto and Jerry, quit that shoving or you can move to the back of the line!"

As the two lines achieve a semblance of form, Mrs. Howard quietly inspects each. "The girls, as usual, are going to get to come in first. Boys, I want you to notice how sweet and quiet these little ladies can be when they want to, and what a nice straight line they can make, too. David and Johnny, your roughhousing is messing up the whole boys' line. Now all the boys will have to wait because you two still don't know how to stand still for 1 minute. Girls, you may come in now."

Throughout the day, the children are given tacit messages about the supposed differences between boys and girls (for example, boys are disobedient, noisy, and express anger with aggressive behaviors; girls are docile, interested in their appearance, and express anger with tears and requests for adult assistance). Arbitrary segregation by sex (such as separate lines for boys and girls, encouragement of same-sex cohorts as primary playmates) cultivates an adversarial, rather than collegial, relationship between the sexes. Teacher expectations and beliefs about appropriate sex roles can have a dramatic effect on children's behavior and attitudes toward those who deviate from traditional norms (for example, girls shouldn't get dirty or enjoy rough play; boys should limit their play in the doll corner to being "daddies"). These practices can promote gender stereotyping and the development of sexist attitudes (Derman-Sparks & the A.B.C. Task Force, 1989; Mischel, 1970; Sprung, 1975) to which children may be particularly susceptible during the early childhood years (Stoddart & Turiel, 1985).

The girls file in and form another line outside the bathroom, where they must wait for a turn to wash their hands. The bathroom is crowded, dingy, and poorly ventilated. The children irritate easily in this unpleasant atmosphere; shoving, pinching, rude remarks, and teacher reprimands are the result. As Alicia and Jody leave the bathroom together, still wiping their hands on paper towels, the boys' line begins to weave into the room. The girls look to Suzanne to see what they are supposed to be doing.

"Alicia and Jody, go sit down at the table with the kindergartners," Suzanne directs; "Minh and Tyrone, you can go over there, too." She turns and calls out, "Marti, Rosa, could you please come over and help these kids get settled at their tables?"

Rosa and Marti are busy whispering together and polishing their fingernails in the back of the room. "Oh, shit, what a total bitch," Marti mumbles as the teenagers rise, both shaking and blowing on their wet fingernails as they slowly trudge across the room.

Alicia sits down between Carlos and Dorette, who look like really big kids to her. She watches in fascination as Latrina opens a book and begins to read aloud, just like a mommy ("Mommy, where's Mommy?" she wonders). Latrina's story is about two little boys who don't want to go to bed. It's funny, and Alicia even smiles a little as the other kids burst into giggles at a really silly part. Just then, Marti leans over and wrenches the book out of Latrina's hands.

"This is the game table, dummy; you're all supposed to be playing games here. No books." Marti tosses the book carelessly over toward the book corner.

"That's *my* book from school," Latrina screams in protest. "I got it from the library!"

"Well, then, put it in your cubbie where it belongs!" Marti replies.

Minh

As Latrina jumps up to retrieve her book, Alicia looks around in dismay. She never played these kinds of games before. Minh is spinning a wheel and juggling some dice in his hands. That looks like fun. Alicia leans across the table and asks, "Can I play that game, too, okay?"

Minh continues to look at the dice in his hand and doesn't respond. Alicia is about to ask him again when Dorette interjects, "He doesn't know how to talk. He's stupid. We don't like him. Look at his haircut. It's *weird*!" At this, they both burst out laughing. "I'll play with you," offers Dorette. "Look, here's *Candyland®*. That's a good one for little kids."

Minh is a new boy from Vietnam. He knows very little English and is quite shy about interacting with the other children. His parents are ignorant about American style and don't realize that the children make fun of his "bowl" haircut and his habit of sometimes wearing pajama tops for shirts. Since his enrollment in the center 6 weeks previously, Minh has remained isolated from any social intercourse with the children. None of the teachers have made any attempt to draw him into the group; in fact, since no one has bothered to get any real assessment of his level of understanding or abilities, he is rarely even encouraged to participate in program activities.

Since the Wee Tots curriculum has no provisions for multicultural education, none of the staff have made any effort to educate the children about how the differences in Minh's appearance and behavior reflect differences in his cultural heritage. This is unfortunate, because the presence of peers with different ethnic origins is an ideal incentive for developing young children's appreciation of multicultural variations in language and lifestyle (Bredekamp, 1987; Derman-Sparks & the A.B.C. Task Force, 1989; Ramsey, 1982).

Going Home

As the children proceed with their "quiet" activities, the staff begins the lengthy end-of-the day maintenance chores required when janitorial help is at a minimum. Rosa and Marti go outside to lock up the sand toys and bikes. Suzanne tackles the bathroom and begins to wash out the sinks and scrub the toilets. Mrs. Howard bustles around the room, straightening up toy shelves and seeing that the children concentrate on their assigned activities so that no further mess is made. Parents arrive with increasing frequency and exchange only peremptory remarks with the staff: "Benny needs more extra clothes in his cubbie, Mrs. Wills; he had an accident at naptime and we had to change him."

Distractedly fiddling with a puzzle, Jerry begins the long wait to go home. All the children seem fidgety and look up expectantly each time the front door opens. It's as though the center is marking time now until the closing bell rings at 6:00. Rosa and Marti wait by the door, watching as the hands of the clock slowly approach the end of their shift. At 5:00, they race, snickering, out the door. Alicia raises her hand to wave goodbye, but the big girls leave without a word or a backward look.

Alicia is tired of sitting at the table with a lot of games that are too hard for her to play. When Mrs. Howard's back is turned, she slips out of her seat and tiptoes over to the doll corner. She ducks into an open cabinet that is supposed to represent the play stove. She reaches out to grab a dolly and a blanket, then closes the door behind her. It is warm and cozy in the cabinet and not too dark, because light is coming in through the holes above her head, which are supposed to look like the burners on the stovetop. At last she is alone, away from all the teasing, yelling voices and angry faces. She closes her eyes and begins to gently rock her baby. She hums a soft lullaby until sleep overwhelms her.

When her shift ends at 5:30, Mrs. Curtis, the preschool teacher from the next room, brings her remaining kids in to end the day with Mrs. Howard. The forlorn group, sweaty in their heavy coats and backpacks, lines up by the door to wait for their parents. At this signal, Mrs. Howard claps her hands and announces to her class, "Okay, it's time for all you kids to clean up your activities and get into your coats and backpacks!" Suzanne shoos the children out of their seats so she can begin to stack the chairs on the tables. Mrs. Howard flits from child to child tying laces and zipping up coats. Mrs. Howard has the end-of-the-day preparations down to a science; she is determined that nothing will prevent her from catching her 6:00 bus.

Mrs. Woodbury, breathless from running all the way from the bus stop, flings open the door and looks around expectantly for Alicia. She scans the rows of tired, waiting faces but fails to locate her daughter's familiar one. "Excuse me, I'm looking for my little girl, Alicia. Do you know where she is?" Mrs. Woodbury asks hopefully as she approaches Suzanne.

"Oh, Alicia." Suzanne hesitates, trying to remember what Alicia looks like. "Well, she must be around here someplace. Let's check with Mrs. Howard." Suzanne calls out to Mrs. Howard, who is consulting with the center's owner-operator, Mr. Proctor, out in the hall. "Mrs. Howard, this lady is looking for her daughter, Alicia. Didn't she already get picked up?"

At this, Mrs. Woodbury hurries across the room to the other adults, panic erupting in her voice as she insists, "Please, where is my daugher? What kind of school *is* this? You have to find Alicia!"

Mr. Proctor brushes past Mrs. Howard and announces in a condescending tone, "Now, now, Mrs. Woodbury, isn't it?" As Mrs. Woodbury nods in reply, Mr. Proctor silently congratulates himself on his fine memory and continues, "Now, I'm sure Alicia has just secreted herself somewhere. You know, children are so playful at this age. Mrs. Howard?"

Mrs. Howard looks at him and nervously rubs her mouth with her hand. "Well, she was just here a minute ago. I'm sure she didn't go out the door." As Mrs. Woodbury gasps at this remark, Mrs. Howard hastily adds, "Mr. Proctor or I would have seen her . . ."

Turning to the class, all of whose eyes are now focused on Mrs. Woodbury's frightened face, Mr. Proctor asks, "Now, boys and girls, one of you must have seen where Alicia went?" When he gets no response, he adds in a sterner tone, "Don't you know where your little friend is? Speak up now, children, so we can all go home when the rest of your parents arrive."

The children look at one another anxiously, not relishing to idea of being held hostage. Tyrone suggests, "Maybe she's in the bathroom." As Mrs. Woodbury and Suzanne race to look, other children begin to offer their ideas.

"Maybe she went outside and got locked in the shed with the bicycles," Jamila pipes up. Mr. Proctor hushes Jamila with a finger to his lips as Mrs. Woodbury returns wild-eyed from the empty bathroom. As tears well up in her eyes, she begins, shakily, to speak, when she notices Minh staring intensely at her. As she returns his cold look, he lifts his arm and points silently to the doll corner.

Mrs. Woodbury sprints across the room, shouting out Alicia's name. At this, dazed and yawning, Alicia emerges from her secret hiding place and mumbles "Oh, hi, Mommy," in a small voice. Mrs. Woodbury rushes to take her in her arms, but Alicia turns her head to repel her mother's embrace.

> It is not unusual for young children to display avoidant be-
> haviors during reunion when they have been separated from
> their parents throughout a long, and in this case traumatic, child
> care day (Schwartz, 1983).

Mrs. Woodbury, ignoring Alicia's protests, lifts her into her arms. She looks glaringly at Mr. Proctor and demands, "I want someone to tell me what you have been doing with my child all day. Her eyes are red and puffy and she looks like she's been asleep for hours! What kind of a program is this when you can't even keep track of the children!" She clutches Alicia, now crying softly, more tightly to her chest.

Mr. Proctor gives Mrs. Woodbury an understanding smile in response, then turns to Mrs. Howard and suggests, "Mrs. Howard, I think Alicia's mother needs some reassurance that you are in complete control of these children throughout the day." Before Mrs. Howard can defend herself, Mr. Proctor continues, "But you know, these little imps can disappear with the blink of an eye. I'm sure when Alicia gets accustomed to the routine here she'll realize how important it is for her to mind her teachers. Won't you, Alicia?" At this he reaches out to give Alicia's head a little pat. Alicia howls in response and burrows her head further into her mother's chest.

Mr. Proctor is now painfully aware of the fact that a number of parents have entered the room and are watching this interchange with intense interest. In one last attempt to diffuse the situation, he takes Mrs. Woodbury by the arm and offers, "Why don't we continue our discussion in my office where we can be more comfortable?"

"I don't think there is anything further to discuss," Mrs. Woodbury snaps. "I'm withdrawing my daughter from your care immediately. And I'll take this matter up with the proper authorities!"

"Now, Mrs. Woodbury, please don't upset yourself. I assure you we're a reputable program and comply with all state regulations."

Ignoring Mr. Proctor's further attempts to subdue her anger, Mrs. Woodbury gathers Alicia's things from her cubbie and storms out the door, Alicia clinging to her neck.

Annie Spinoza, Jerry's mom, sighs as she watches the Woodburys depart. She gives her son a big hug, hoping that what she just witnessed was really just the ravings of a hysterical mother. As she steers Jerry toward the door, Annie gives Mr. Proctor a little nod. She feels reassured, seeing how he is calmly smiling and chatting with the parents who surround him, all wanting to speculate on the "scene" Mrs. Woodbury created. Annie muses to herself, "After all, Mr. Proctor is a child care professional; he must know what he's doing. And anyway, where else could I take Jerry? I can't quit my job, and this is the most reasonable care in town . . ."

Jerry, wishing desperately that his mom felt the same way as Alicia's, silently follows his mother out into the approaching night.

3
Second Step
Children's Center

BACKGROUND

Second Step Children's Center is a small, private, nonprofit early childhood program serving children from 1 to 5 years of age. It is located in a quiet, working-class, residential neighborhood on the outskirts of the same city as Wee Tots Nursery School and Day Care. The center is housed in a remodeled home. It consists of a preschool area that serves sixteen 3- to 5-year-olds per day with two staff (1:8 adult-child ratio) and an infant-toddler area that serves six 1- and 2-year-olds per day with a staff of two (1:3 ratio). The ratio for the preschoolers is enriched considerably by the addition of a teaching assistant who works across the busy morning hours and an afternoon extended-care teacher whose hours overlap with those of the regular staff during the transitional afternoon period, lowering the ratio to 1:5.3 throughout the bulk of the learning day.

Ratio, Group Size, and Program Structure

Second Step's ratios and group sizes are similar to those proposed by the Federal Interagency Day Care Requirements (FIDCR) (Clarke-Stewart, 1982; Scarr, 1984) and the National Academy of Early Childhood Programs (National Association for the Education of Young Children, 1984), as well as to the ratios required and the group sizes recommended by the California State Department of Education (SDE) for it's state-funded child-care centers (Grubb, 1989).

Eighteen children are enrolled in Second Step's preschool classroom, with 16 children in attendance on any given day. Although most preschoolers attend the program 5 days per week, families are given

58

the option of scheduling 3 or 4 specific days per week if that alternative better meets their work or study needs. The basic hours of operation are from 9:00 A.M. to 4:00 P.M. each day, with extended care from 8:00 to 9:00 A.M. and/or from 4:00 to 5:30 P.M.

The staff feel strongly that most preschoolers fare best in group care for no longer than about a 7-hour day, regardless of the quality of the program. Thus Second Step's basic program runs from 9:00 A.M. to 4:00 P.M., although most parents are employed for longer hours. Parents are encouraged to seek more flexibility in their own schedules so that children can benefit from early morning and late afternoon times at home; therefore, many families have arranged alternating work schedules. For example, Yvette's mother, Cindy Brenner, drops her off at 9:00 and then works until 6:00, while Yvette's dad, Jim, goes to his teaching job at 7:00 and picks up Yvette by 4:00. Alberto's dad, Martin Garcia, works a traditional 9:00 to 5:00 day, but Alberto's mom, Elena, is involved in a job-share and finds it most convenient to enroll Alberto 3 full days per week with extended care and stay home with him on the other 2 days.

For other parents such as Jerry's mom, Annie Spinoza, who is a single mother, an abbreviated child care schedule is simply not feasible. These families, who make up about 20 percent of the enrollment, require both morning and afternoon extended care 5 days per week. The staff makes a special effort to see that these extended care hours are nurturing and homelike so as to ensure each child a warm and peaceful beginning and end to a long school day.

The program requires parents to participate for the equivalent of 2 hours per month. Parents can choose from a variety of participation tasks: some volunteer in the classroom on a regular basis, others come in once or twice a year to work on projects such as a yard cleanup day or repainting the bookshelves in the classroom, others contribute their skills by working at home to complete needed tasks (such as repairing broken toys and torn books, sewing sheets for the cots), and still others serve on the Parent Advisory Committee or the Fund-Raising Committee, which organizes the program's yearly fund-raising events in which all families participate. Parent participation has been a successful way of both involving parents in the day-to-day life of the center and providing needed assistance without raising fees.

A more significant source of funding is provided by a special endowment which provides at least partial fee subsidies to most families using the center. These outside resources make it possible for an ethnically and economically diverse group of children to benefit from Second Step's excellent program.

The Staff

There are four staff who care for the preschoolers in Second Step: Louise, Tom, and Jackie are teachers; Juanita is the student teaching assistant. Although Second Step is privately funded, all the teachers hold either a California teaching credential or a Children's Center Instructional Permit, certification that also authorizes teaching in a state-subsidized child development program. (The credential requires 1 year of post-baccalaureate training; the permit requires teaching experience, a minimum of 24 units in child development or early childhood education, 16 units of general college education courses, passage of a basic skills test, and continuing education for those who do not hold a bachelor's degree.)

All teachers are certified in pediatric first aid and CPR. Louise, a co-founder of Second Step, is its assistant director. She holds an elementary teaching credential with an early childhood emphasis, a Children's Center Supervision Permit, and a recently completed master's degree in early childhood education. She taught kindergarten in the public schools for 6 years and then taught preschool in a California state-subsidized children's center for another 4 years before co-founding Second Step 8 years ago. Louise is currently enrolled in a course in conversational Spanish. She hopes to improve her bilingual skills in order to better serve the increasing number of Hispanic children attending the program.

Tom had just finished his B.A. in music when he first came to Second Step 5 years ago. He was originally hired as a music resource teacher to do a series of workshops for the staff. (These and other in-service training activities are paid for through the staff training budget, the existence of which demonstrates the seriousness of the program's commitment to the continuing education of its staff.) Tom then became a substitute teacher at Second Step and several other local preschools. He was first hired as a teaching assistant while he was completing the additional units in early childhood education and child development that he needed to obtain his Children's Center Instructional Permit, although he asserts that his real training in early childhood is due in great part to Louise's skilled supervision of his work during that period of internship.

Jackie, the afternoon and extended care teacher, taught in a variety of preschool settings for several years before settling into her present position at Second Step 3 years ago. She holds a Children's Center Instructional Permit and, although she is not currently interested in completing her B.A., continues to take college-level courses in early childhood education and art.

Juanita is Second Step's morning teaching assistant. She is studying child development at a local college and is supervised in her field experience at Second Step by Louise. Juanita receives a work-study award from her college, so only a portion of her wages is paid by the program. Second Step is committed to maintaining a training position in each classroom in order to provide opportunities for future teachers to receive their training in a high-quality, developmentally appropriate early childhood program. The teaching staff benefits as well, from the fresh perspectives and enthusiasm that the trainees bring with them. It is important to note here, though, that this training position is both functional and effective because it is used to *enrich* an already strong and stable program rather than to *replace* core staff members with less expensive unskilled labor.

Staff Training

The program's insistence on hiring caregivers with extensive experience and child-related training is supported by research that confirms that children's social, cognitive, and language development benefit accordingly (e.g., Berk, 1985; Howes, 1983; Ruopp et al., 1979). Equally important, though, is how teachers utilize this training in their interactions with children.

Teachers must be able to support optimal development in all areas, not just the intellectual. Sometimes even teachers with specialized training in early childhood education tend to focus on children's cognitive development and see their role as one of preparing children for academic learning through adult-directed activities and instruction. It is crucial that these caregivers also develop skills in promoting the overall development of the whole child, supporting children's self-directed play in positive, stimulating, and responsive ways (Almy, 1982). Second Step's teachers eschew the use of traditional instructional strategies, instead focusing on setting up the learning environment so that children can choose freely from among activities that are inherently interesting to them, that encourage the elaboration of their thinking, and that involve them actively with adults, peers, and materials.

Louise, Tom, and Jackie continue to benefit from comprehensive early childhood training activities that enable them to link current research and theories of development to educational practices that encompass all areas of development. "Teachers need to learn how child development principles can be applied in everything they do with children, including managing daily routines of napping or mealtime, facilitating play, arranging the physical environment, and guiding children's behavior" (Logue, Eheart, & Leavitt, 1986, p. 9). In fact, several recent studies have shown an alarming link between negative social behaviors and children's enrollment in academically oriented early childhood programs that emphasize direct instruction over child-initiated learning (Haskins, 1985; Schweinhart, Weikart, & Larner, 1986). To counteract these effects, the Second Step program emphasizes social and emotional development as a central theme of its curriculum.

Staff Compensation, Working Conditions, and Stability

All the teachers at Second Step are paid on a salary schedule, with rewards for both continuing education and years of service. They receive full health benefits and generous paid leave time for sickness and vacations. Even though Second Step's salaries and benefits are among the highest in their local child care community, they are still not comparable with those earned in the local public schools. Achieving salary parity remains a goal for the program, but it remains virtually a pipe dream without additional sources of funding to supplement the already substantial parent fees.

Tom and Louise each work a 7-hour shift that includes one morning break and a 45-minute break for lunch. Each is also paid for an additional hour of "prep time" per day, which includes recordkeeping, observation of the children, conferring with parents, staff meetings, planning curriculum, attending child development and early education workshops, and other related training. Jackie works a part-time shift and receives compensation and benefits that correspond to her shorter shift.

Staff compensation at Second Step is by far the most expensive component of the program, but it is also the most important. The National Child Care Staffing Study (Whitebook, Howes, & Phillips, 1989) recently demonstrated that, among the adult work environment variables they measured, staff salary is the most important predictor of the quality of care that children receive. Good salaries, benefits, and working conditions attract highly qualified caregivers who are likely to remain in their positions (Whitebook et al., 1981; Whitebook et al., 1989; Willer, 1987).

Caregiver stability, availability, and predictability all strengthen attachment formation, a central feature of a child's healthy adjustment to the child care setting. Research confirms that children do get attached to their caregivers and use them as a secure base to return to throughout the day (Cummings, 1980). Children exhibit more positive affect and interact more with stable caregivers (Cummings, 1980; Rubenstein & Howes, 1979). Staff continuity is also positively related to children's cognitive and social development (Clarke-Stewart & Gruber, 1984; Kontos & Fiene, 1987). The National Child Care Staffing Study (Whitebook et al., 1989) reports that "children in centers with higher turnover rates spent less time engaged in social activities with peers and more time in Aimless Wandering" (p. 12). These children also scored lower on language development tests when compared with children in centers with more stable staff.

The loss of these attachment figures can be devastating to young children, especially when the annual staff turnover rate among center-based child care programs exceeds 40 percent (National Association for the Education of Young Children, 1985b; Whitebook et al., 1989). "The child who experiences many different caregivers may not become attached to any of them and thus will fail to be secure in child care. . . . The child who forms attachments to a series of caregivers, all of whom leave, may find it too painful to continue the cycle and conclude that human relationships are to be avoided" (Howes, 1987, p. 82).

STORY

Arrival

When 5-year-old Jerry Spinoza arrives at Second Step each morning around 8:00, his teacher, Louise, always jumps up to greet him with a hearty "Good morning!" and a big hug. He also gets a happy greeting from Juanita, the morning teaching assistant, and "Hi" and "Jerry's here!" from the other children already busily at play. As he hangs up his coat in the cozy cubbie corner near the door, he scans the other 15 cubbies to check whose coats have arrived ahead of his. "Great, Jamila's here today," he thinks to himself, happy at the return of his good friend who was out with a cold the previous day.

Even for a child care "pro" like Jerry, who has been at Second Step since he was a baby, the morning transition from home to school is a sensitive time. The staff make a point of ensuring that each child receives a warm welcome and is allowed to start the day off in a manner that suits his or her individual style. For example, some children need time to stay close to their parents or remain in the cubbie area before moving into the group. Others, like Jerry, like to plunge right into an activity. These individual differences are supported and accommodated by good early childhood programs (Bredekamp, 1987; Greenman, 1988).

As Jerry bounces out of the cubbie corner, he looks with interest at what the other children are doing. He notices that four other children have arrived so far this morning. Minh, Katie, and Latosha are kneading playdough with Juanita, while Jamila is relaxing on the rug in the book corner with a pile of books by her side.

The room, though quite large, is warm and inviting. Low shelves, focused soft incandescent lighting, and subtle variations in texture and color are used to define separate areas. All the walls at child eye level are covered with the children's most recently completed work: paintings, collages, dictated stories. A pottery shelf displays the children's latest clay and wood sculptures. Jerry smiles when he notices that one of the teachers has hung his "SA Dw" (Save the Whales) sign above the science display shelf. At present, only the book corner and the table area are fully illuminated. As more children arrive, the teachers will open each area to accommodate the children's fluctuating energies and interests.

The book corner is in a central area of the room. It is carpeted in a mellow beige tweed, which was selected for both its sturdiness and its softness. The rug is bounded on one side by a piano that faces a low, rose-colored couch. Several thin rectangular pillows, covered in a washable, leaf-colored velour, are available for sitting on or leaning against the piano legs during circle time. At the wall end of the rug, two birch book display stands each put 5 rows of picture books within easy reach of rug sitters. Only 15 to 20 books are displayed on each stand at any time, so that their cheerful covers will be fully visible and enticing to the young readers.

The books, all in excellent condition, are rotated each week or two through the program's extensive library of children's literature, the bulk of which is stored in a large bookcase in the parent-teacher room just behind the cubbie area. Each book was carefully selected for its developmental appropriateness as well as for the quality of its illustrations and the language used (Oppenheim, Brenner, & Boegehold, 1986). The library also includes educational journals, teacher resource books, and books on a variety of child-related topics, such as child development, nutrition, and parenting issues. Anyone affiliated with the program—teachers, parents, and children—has library privileges and can take a favorite book home at any time.

Approximately two-thirds of the center's floor area is carpeted. The remaining third is covered in a springy beige linoleum. This is the eating and art area of the room. There are three small, round, wooden tables with matching chairs in two sizes to accommodate variations in children's height. During activity times throughout the day, there is always a group of children in this area, busily at work on a daily art project set up by a teacher, or inventing an art project of their own using a variety of supplies that are always left within their reach in the "do-it-yourself corner." These include various kinds and sizes of good-quality paper, and envelopes (for "writing" letters); pencils, crayons, oil pastels, and markers in excellent condition; glue sticks; playdough with accessories for cutting or molding; collage materials; crafts materials (wood, yarn, feathers, and so forth); safety scissors (for both right- and left-handers); and child-sized staplers.

Early in the year, the staff takes special time to introduce the children to the variety of materials available in the do-it-yourself area. The children are encouraged to use these supplies independently (or with the assistance of peers) whenever they "feel like making something." The materials are organized for easy clean-up, and the children are expected to clean up after themselves as best they can (Bredekamp, 1987; Greenman, 1988; Harms & Clifford, 1980; Lasky & Mukerji, 1980).

Jerry makes a point of giving Jamila a special smile and then takes a seat at the playdough table. He begins to happily squish the bright orange clay between his fingers. "Jerry, look at the new color Juanita made this morning!" offers Katie in an excited voice. She hands Jerry a big blob of yellow-green playdough.

"Oooh, what kinda color is dis?" Jerry wonders aloud in his baby talk voice, poking the blob with a tongue depressor. "It's kinda weird, like shlime." The other children giggle and begin a discussion about whether the color is really yellow or green.

"It's a Ghostbusters' color!" Katie suggests.

"Like dragon," adds Minh with a shy smile.

"Me could call it yellowy-gween or gweeny-yellow," says Jerry, proud of his facile use of language, baby talk and all.

"This color also has a French name," Juanita offers. "It's called 'chartreuse,' after a drink that comes from France."

"Cartwoose," laughs Jerry, "shounds dike a cartoon show!" The children burst into giggles once again.

"Shartooth? I don' wanna drink that stuff! Hurts my teeth!" announces 3½-year-old Latosha, displaying her gums in a big grimace. "I gonna make me a shartooth dragon with big fat shartooth teeth!"

"Yeah," agrees Jerry, "and you could use da orange to make fire coming out of his mouf! Me gonna make one, too!"

> Juanita allows the laughter and word play to continue. She has come to understand that language play enhances language development, sensitizing children to the richness of linguistic forms and encouraging imagination and invention (Bredekamp, 1987; Cazden, 1981a).

A Worried Parent

As Jerry eases himself into another full day with his preschool classmates, his mom, Annie Spinoza, hangs her purse and coat on the parent coatrack and then completes the daily sign-in sheet that rests on the shelf above. The sheet includes an area for parents to alert staff to any special needs their child might have that day and to give the staff authorization for administering any prescribed medications, and an area for teachers to leave individualized messages for the parents at the end of the day. As Annie writes, Louise joins her and reads Annie's comments. Seeing that Jerry and the others are busily absorbed in play, they take a few minutes to sit down on a window seat to exchange further information.

> Second Step's generous teacher-child ratio makes it possible for a teacher to spend a few minutes with each child and his or her parent upon arrival each day. Because the teachers here see themselves in partnership with parents, this regular communication at the beginning and the end of the day promotes a shared understanding of how the child's day-to-day experiences relate to his or her overall development.
>
> To maintain consistency in their interactions with each child, the teachers pass on relevant information about the children to one another throughout the day and, in greater depth, at the weekly staff meetings. In turn, parents are kept up-to-date on the staff's observations of and interactions with their children. In addition, center policy requires regular parent conferences with the child's special teacher as well as informal conferences that are held at either parent or teacher request. In

this way, teachers and parents work together to consolidate the child's world by smoothing the ongoing transition between home and center (Bredekamp, 1987; Clarke-Stewart, 1982; Powell, 1980; Scarr, 1984).

Annie Spinoza expresses concern about her son's recent irritability and mischievous behaviors. "And, what's worse, Jerry even announced at dinner last night that he hates kindergarten and doesn't ever want to go there!"

"You know," Louise responds, "Jerry's not the only one. We've been seeing a lot more agitation and restlessness lately among the 4- and 5-year-olds like Jerry who are getting ready to enter kindergarten in a few months. I think a lot of what we're seeing with these kids is really fear—fear of the unknown, because they really know very little yet about what kindergarten is really like and have probably all heard some frightening tales about strict teachers and mean bullies and stuff like that."

"Well, you know, that's interesting," Annie replies with a thoughtful frown, "because I heard Jerry telling his little cousin just the other day that you have to be able to *read* to go to kindergarten. I wonder if he's worried about that, since he's not nearly ready to read yet. I never said anything because I just thought he was just bragging to his cousin about how grown-up he's getting. I guess I better talk to him some more about all this and reassure him that nobody needs to know how to read in kindergarten!"

"Right!" Louise agrees. "Because even though Jerry knows what it means to be successful and fit in happily here, he might really be afraid of not doing well in kindergarten. I know that kids often worry about all kinds of things that they're sometimes hesitant to express to grown-ups. What you're telling me makes me realize that we should probably schedule our field trip to Vendola School a bit earlier than usual this year. You know, Mrs. Kendall, the kindergarten teacher there, gives the children a wonderful tour of her room, shows the neat projects the children get to make, lets them tour the cafeteria and library, and answers all the kids' questions about kindergarten. The children always enjoy their visit tremendously and generally seem to feel a lot more positive about being kindergartners after that experience."

"That sounds like something Jerry would really enjoy. But, also, is there anything you think we can do at home to help the situation?" asks Annie.

"Well, first off, it helps a lot that you're telling me all this because we can begin to connect what you're seeing at home with what we're seeing here. It might be great for Jerry if you all could begin to talk at home—positively, of course—about what his kindergarten days are likely to be like. Let him know how proud you are of the way he's growing up and of all his new interests and abilities."

"Well, you really are right about that. I guess I've been so upset with his bad attitude lately and now this baby talk—I've really been on his case a lot about that."

"Now *that* is perfectly understandable," Louise laughs, "and I guarantee you that you're not the only parent of a prekindergartner who's tearing her hair out this time of year! And by the way, the baby talk is very popular now with all of Jerry's buddies and is something we see just about every year." Annie gives Louise a relieved look, and the two of them watch the children quietly engaged in play.

After a few moments pass, Louise continues. "A couple of the other parents have mentioned that they've been taking their kids on visits to the school grounds in the evenings or on weekends to play in the kindergarten yard and to peek in the windows. I think Jerry might enjoy that, too. You could also remind him which of his old friends will be joining him this fall—you know, there will be eight of them going, so he can remember that he won't be all alone in this new and exciting experience. Oh, and this all makes *me* realize that *I* need to remind all our big kids that even though they'll be going off to kindergarten soon, they will *always* be a special part of our Second Step family!"

"Thanks, Louise," Annie says, as she reaches around Louise's broad shoulder to give her a little hug. "You always know how to make me feel better!"

"Hey, you've got a great kid there—although he does have his moments!" Louise replies with a wink. "Well, I should really get back to the kids now, and I know you have to get to work." Annie nods, and they both rise from the window seat. As they walk toward the children, Louise concludes, "Let's check back on this soon, Annie. And, remember, if you want to talk further, we can always schedule a conference."

This exchange demonstrates the importance of several key abilities of the good early childhood educator. First, Louise's years of experience working with this age group, coupled with her careful observation skills, enable her to make a reasonable hypothesis about the origin of Jerry's recent irritable behaviors. She has come to understand that many children this age become anxious as the transition to kindergarten approaches. She knows that this anxiety often manifests itself in behaviors sim-

ilar to those Jerry and some of his friends are exhibiting at
school. By consulting with Jerry's mom, she is able to identify a
pattern of behavior that confirms her suspicions. Louise's sympathetic and knowledgeable responses to Annie's concerns
soothe Annie's worries and involve her as an essential partner in
easing the impact of the approaching transition (Bredekamp,
1987).

The staff at Second Step recognize the importance of advance preparation on the part of teachers and parents to ensure
that the child's transition from preschool to kindergarten is a
positive experience. They work collaboratively with the kindergarten teachers at the local public schools to familiarize themselves, the children, and their parents with the kind of educational program their graduates will be entering. Young children's
expectations about their roles as students and about the
teacher's role may need to be substantially modified in light of
the realities of the particular new setting (Klein, 1988; Klein,
Kantor, & Fernie, 1988; Reifel, 1988).

Equally important, the kindergarten teachers are, in turn,
made aware of the nature of the developmental program and
the range of activities and concepts their incoming students
have experienced at Second Step. Continuity between early
childhood programs is a key element in supporting the child's
continued success through the elementary years (Bredekamp,
1987; National Association of State Boards of Education, 1988).

Alberto

As Annie Spinoza gets up to say goodbye to Jerry, Louise feels a
gentle tapping on her leg. She looks up to see 3-year-old Alberto, who
is motioning her to follow him.

"Good morning, Alberto, I didn't see you come in!" Alberto takes
Louise by the hand and leads her to where his mom, Elena, is hanging
his coat in his cubbie. Alberto points to a stuffed owl sitting in his
cubbie.

"He brought it for sharing," Elena says in an apologetic tone. "I
told him sharing time wasn't till tomorrow, but he was so excited to
show it to you. His uncle brought it with him from Colombia last
night."

Louise kneels down to speak, in Spanish, at eye level with Alberto.
"Alberto, we would really like for you to share your owl today. I know
that having your uncle come from Colombia is very special for you.
The children will want to hear all about it, so you can do a special
sharing time today." Alberto smiles and hands his owl to Louise. She

takes it gently, gives it a nice hug, and says in English, "Hello, Owl, welcome to Second Step!" Elena looks both pleased and relieved.

Louise knows that Alberto, who speaks only Spanish at home, is still often reluctant to speak English at school. The staff has decided to put no pressure on Alberto to converse in English until he is ready. Their observations of his ability to respond appropriately to both English- and Spanish-speaking peers and caregivers indicate that Alberto's comprehension in both languages is steadily improving. They are confident that he will begin to speak more when he has something he really wants to say (Gonzalez-Mena, 1981).

Louise is encouraged by Alberto's interest in sharing his owl today. She is happy to make an exception to the "Wednesday is sharing day" rule in order to support Alberto's enthusiasm to communicate to his friends *something that is important to him*. Louise's gesture is not simply kindness on her part, but an affirmation of the program's philosophy that teachers' needs to maintain regularity in the daily schedule must periodically yield to individual children's needs to function outside those routines (Bredekamp, 1987).

Minh

Annie Spinoza takes a moment to join Jerry at the playdough table before saying goodbye. She admires the "dragon castle" that Jerry is now busily constructing with his old friend, Jamila, and a newer friend, Minh.

Juanita looks up from the couch, where she is snuggled between Latosha and Katie, reading from a pile of books the girls have selected. "'Bye now, Annie, have a great day at work! Let me know when you put those red shoes on sale. I want 'em!"

Annie smiles, gives Jerry one last kiss, and heads off for a long day as manager of a local shoe store. As she turns to go, Minh lifts his head and whispers, "'Bye, 'bye." Annie and Juanita give one another delighted looks. Bidding goodbye to a parent is a first for Minh.

Minh is a Southeast Asian refugee with a limited command of English. Since his arrival 6 weeks previously, the staff has made a concerted effort to assess his level of understanding and abilities and to integrate him into the social world of the group. After interviewing his family at length, with the help of a county-provided interpreter, the teachers discovered that Minh is especially interested in constructing models but is also quite shy and withdrawn. They used this information to plan activities that would be likely to arouse his interest and allow him a nonverbal means of communicating his special talents and interests to his peers. The children were quickly impressed with Minh's skills and now include him quite comfortably in their play. He, in turn, is learning English rapidly from his new friends.

The teachers also gathered information about life in Vietnam and, with the help of his parents, had a special circle time in which Minh's classmates were introduced to the customs, food, clothes, music, and language of their new friend's native country. In turn, the other children each told Minh something about their own American culture. This last step is extremely important, for without mutual sharing of information, there is a tacit implication that the American way is the "real" way, with the ways of other cultures seen as interesting, but inferior, models. By encouraging children to appreciate differences in cultural heritage, teachers foster an understanding of and respect for multicultural variations in lifestyle, language, and appearance (Bredekamp, 1987; Derman-Sparks & the A.B.C. Task Force, 1989; Ramsey, 1982).

Breakfast—Cinnamon Toast

At 8:30, the early birds are served breakfast. This is a simple meal, prepared in the kitchen by Louise or Juanita. The kitchen counter is really a big window opening into the playroom. Here, the children can climb up on stools and converse with the cook.

"Whatcha makin' today, Juanita?" asks Latosha. "I want pancakes."

"Well, it's not pancakes, but it's something really yummy that you're gonna like!" she replies, sprinkling cinnamon-sugar over some thick pieces of toast.

"What's that thing?" asks Jerry as he climbs up on the other stool.

"It's a shaker; see the holes where stuff comes out?"

"Well, what's in it?"

"It's cinnamon and sugar mixed together," Juanita replies. Seeing Jerry's vague look, she offers, "Here, wanna smell it? Cinnamon has a neat smell."

"What about the sugar?" asks Jerry, taking a sniff. "How does *it* smell?"

"Gosh, I don't really know. Why don't we smell some! Here, I'll put some in a separate bowl." Juanita scoops some plain sugar into a little bowl. Then, as an afterthought, she sprinkles some cinnamon into another. She puts both bowls on the counter in front of the children.

"That cinnamon sure is powdery," comments Jerry as he watches the brown dust mist above the bowl.

"Yeah, *powdery* is a good word, Jerry, sort of like reddish-brown baby powder."

"We don't use that kind on *my* baby's butt," Latosha comments.

"Oh, of course not, Latosha, I only meant it *looks* like baby powder; actually it's a spice called cinnamon." Since Latosha gives her an interested look, Juanita goes on. "Spices make things taste better."

"Lemme taste it," says Latosha, her mouth poised above the bowl.

"Okay, you can each dip a finger in, just once, and get a taste."

"That cimminen is yukky, but that sugar is mmm-mm good!" Latosha declares with a grin.

"Somehow I knew you'd like that sugar, Latosha," Juanita teases. "Your momma told me how you're always trying to get her to buy you those sugary cereals on the TV!" Latosha giggles and quickly dips her finger in the sugar one more time. "Oooh, you're a sneaky one, miss!" Juanita scolds as she whisks the bowls out of reach.

"Oh, do you get Smurf Magic Berries, Latosha?" Jerry asks with a wistful look. "I had those once at my cousin's." His voice trails off as he recalls the pleasures of forbidden sweets.

"I gonna get me those dimestore ones, like on Muppets!" Latosha replies with a smug look. "They're *really* not scary," she adds.

"You mean a cereal you saw on 'Sesame Street,' Latosha?" Juanita translates, then quickly corrects herself. "Oh, no, I guess it would be 'Muppet Babies': there aren't any commercials on 'Sesame Street'. Hmm, 'scary dimestore ones' . . . 'dimestore' . . . dine-saur . . ." Then, enunciating extra clearly, Juanita asks Latosha, "You mean the cereal had little *dinosaurs* in it?"

"Yeah," Latosha responds, "pink ones, and yellow ones, and"—she pauses in thought—"I can't kimember." Then her face breaks out into a grin, "and shartooth ones!"

"Latosha!" Juanita cries with delight. "You remembered the color of our playdough—chartreuse, or 'shartooth' as you like to call it! Good memory!" Juanita leans over the counter to give Latosha a little hug; Latosha responds with a big, proud grin.

Turning back to Jerry, Juanita inquires, "So, anyway, Jerry, what do *you* think?" Jerry thoughtfully licks the last crystals of sugar from his fingers. "About our taste test?"

"Well, I knew that sugar was gonna taste good, but how come this stuff's not sweet?" Jerry wonders, pointing to the cinnamon.

"Well, cinnamon's not really sweet unless you mix it with something sweet, like sugar or honey. It's the mixing together that gives it that special taste." Juanita glances up at the clock. "Uh oh, look at the time! Now you two scoot along and wash your hands and you'll get a chance to taste this special cinnamon toast in a minute!"

What appears to be an ordinary, unremarkable conversation between teacher and children can actually be seen as paradigmatic of an essential difference between high- and low-quality early childhood programs. We know from research on language development that a child's facility with language blossoms in a context where there is opportunity for the child to make a sustained contribution in a dialogue with an adult (not just answering "yes" or "no"). Typically, these opportunities occur most frequently in a healthy home setting where the child's trusting, intimate relationship with a parent gives rise to sustained conversations that focus adult speech on what is of real concern to the child (Tizard, 1981).

In a custodial care setting or in many traditional nursery school environments, teachers are inhibited, by structure or design, from engaging in relaxed, meaningful conversations with individual children. These restrictions include high adult-child ratios, large group size, and the limited range of acceptable topics of conversation in these settings. High staff turnover and lack of staffing continuity complicate the situation by significantly narrowing the teachers' knowledge of individual children. Thus not only are caregivers ignorant of the child's life outside of school, but they are also unaware of any of the child's activities in school that happen to take place outside their range of vision (Cazden, 1981b; Tizard, 1981).

At Second Step, the staff makes it a point to get to know each child, both in school and home contexts, as well as possible. To this end, Tom and Louise visit their special kids' homes at least once a year and maintain an ongoing exchange of information with parents. This communication is especially important with the younger children, whose limited vocabularies, idiosyncratic pronunciations, and egocentric speech require interpretation by someone familiar with the context and content of their communications. The teachers are sensitive to cultural and personal styles of conversing as well. Information thus garnered makes it possible to meaningfully integrate aspects of the child's experience into the daily discourse (Cazden, 1981b; Genishi, 1988). Further, because of the intimate, homelike nature of the program, a richer range of topics for conversation is generated. Cooking, shopping, cleaning, baby care, favorite TV shows, and other topics that have meaning to the children occur as naturally in adult-child discussions here as do topics that arise out of the curriculum (Genishi, 1988; Tizard, 1981).

The New Girl

After breakfast, Louise turns on the other lights, which fully illuminate all corners of the playroom. Since it is nearly 9:00, the rest of the children will soon be arriving. The early birds move out into the room to pursue whatever activities they choose. Louise helps Latosha put on a smock so she can paint at the easel. She looks up to see that Alicia Woodbury, the newest child in the program, and her mother have arrived. Even though Alicia has been spending some time at Second Step for the past 2 weeks, this is her first full day of regular child care. Louise knows that they will both be feeling a bit apprehensive and hurries over to make them feel welcome.

> High-quality programs like Second Step have a well-thought-out set of procedures to facilitate the smooth transition of new children and their families into the center. Parents are encouraged to visit with their children on several occasions before regular child care begins. Teachers emphasize the importance of the parents' reassuring presence during the child's introduction to the program, especially when it is the child's first group-care experience. Parents are asked to stay with their child for decreasing amounts of time during these visits as the child begins to adapt to the idea that the center is "my special place, not mom's or dad's." Skilled caregivers, understanding that parents will be anxious, encourage them to check in often during these sometimes difficult first days or weeks. They know that these initial separations are easier for children whose parents are enthusiastic about the situation, feel comfortable with the staff, and have confidence in the quality of the program (Balaban, 1985; McCracken, 1986).

"Hi, here we are," Virginia Woodbury greets Louise a bit nervously. "We came a bit early, as you suggested."

"Great, that will give Alicia a chance to settle in before the rest of the children come barreling in!" Turning to Alicia, Louise says warmly, "Good morning, Alicia, we're very happy that you're going to be joining us today. We've got some special fun things planned for today that I know you're going to enjoy. Would you like to put your coat in your cubbie? Do you remember where it is?" Alicia nods but doesn't head for her cubbie, so Louise adds, "I see you brought your lion friend again today. Is his name Jimmy?" Alicia nods again and Louise continues, "You know, he doesn't have to stay in your cubbie if you don't want him to. It's okay for him to stay with you today if you like."

Alicia looks relieved. Her battered stuffed lion, Jimmy, is very special to her, and she wants very much for him to stay with her today.

> Louise realizes that the lion is an important transitional object for Alicia. She understands that objects like Alicia's lion, Alberto's stuffed owl, and Bryan's ragged "blankee" are significant because they enable the children to carry a tangible reminder of home along with them to school. These nonsocial attachment objects serve to comfort and reassure children as they move from complete dependence on a primary caregiver to increasing independence. They are especially important during stressful transitions, such as from home to school or during naptime (Balaban, 1985; Jalongo, 1987).

Holding her mother's hand, Alicia wanders over to the large wooden dollhouse that she enjoyed playing with last week. The dollhouse sits on the rug below a large bay window through which the morning sun is shining. It is a warm, enclosing spot that makes Alicia feel cozy and secure. Virginia Woodbury sits on the windowseat and watches her daughter play. Soon Alicia is joined by Alberto, who is carrying his stuffed owl.

"Oh, you have a owl," Alicia says in a friendly voice. Alberto doesn't look at her or respond, so Alicia looks to her mother for assistance. Having been introduced to each of the children last week, Virginia is able to help.

"Remember, this is Alberto, sweetie, maybe he'd like to see Jimmy," Virginia suggests.

"Look, Alberto," Alicia waves to get his attention. "I got this lion. Jimmy." She holds out Jimmy for Alberto to touch. Alberto holds out his owl and the two animals meet in a mock kiss. The children smile shyly at each other, then sit down to play, each happily moving the dollhouse people through the rooms of their well-furnished home.

> The staff understand that all young children, but especially 3-year-olds, need times and places in a group-care situation to play alone or with one or two other children (Bredekamp, 1987; Greenman, 1988). For this reason, the large playroom is designed so that there are several small enclosures that are visible for teacher supervision, but that allow individual children an

opportunity to slip away from the larger group for a bit to
enjoy solitary or intimate play (Harms & Clifford, 1980).

Louise joins Virginia, who expresses some concern about the fact
that the children don't seem to be playing together. Louise comments
in a low voice that 3-year-olds are often happiest playing next to,
instead of actively with, a peer (parallel play). Virginia smiles her
understanding, then stands up to go. Louise reminds her in a low voice
about the goodbye routine they had discussed the week before.

"Right," responds Virginia with a conspiratorial look. She reviews
the process in a whisper: "I'll tell Alicia that I'll be returning to pick her
up right after afternoon snack. And I'll try not to prolong the goodbye
even if Alicia protests. I do realize that dragging out the goodbyes
would just make the separation harder for both of us" (McCracken,
1986).

Louise joins Alicia on the rug as her mother waves good-bye. She
waits quietly as Alicia waves in return and follows every step of her
mom's departure with her eyes. As the realization that her mother is
really gone sinks in, Alicia begins to cry a little. Louise is there to
comfort her and affirm the validity of her feelings. "I know you miss
Mommy right now, Alicia, but she'll be back before you know it.
Meanwhile, Tom and I will be here with you all day. And whenever
you're feeling sad, we'll try to help you feel better. Okay, then?" To
Alicia's shaky nod, Louise goes on, "Now, let's see what's happening
here in this dollhouse. Did you notice that the dolls even have a
microwave oven in their kitchen? Pretty fancy house!"

"We gots a mikawave," Alicia responds with interest. "It goes,
'Ding!' Food's ready!"

"Neat!" Louise comments. "What sound do you think the dolls'
microwave might make when *their* food is all cooked?"

"How 'bout 'Pop, pop'?" Alicia suggests. Alicia and Louise both
turn in surprise as Alberto bursts into giggles, repeating, "Pop, pop.
Pop, pop."

The Playhouse

Tom, the other full-time teacher, arrives and stores his belongings
in his closet in the parent-staff room. He pours himself a cup of coffee
and takes a moment to look through the observation window that
gives onto the classroom. The one-way glass allows parents and
teachers to observe the children's interactions with objects and people
without their presence altering the nature of the play.

Tom quickly scans the room to see if Louise has made any changes in the morning's arrangement of materials that they had agreed on the previous day. He surveys the morning's activity and is pleased to see that everyone appears to be happily engaged in play. He takes a closer look at Katie, who is lying on the rug in the book corner idly flipping the pages of a book. He remarks to himself, "I better check the sign-in sheet to see if anything's going on with Katie; that's awfully quiet for her so early in the morning."

As Tom reenters the classroom to begin his day with the children, the front door opens and Luis, Yvette, and little Nessa all race in at the same time. As their parents chat by the sign-in table, Bryan comes in clinging to his mother's leg. Although Bryan has been at the center since the previous fall, he still has a hard time making the morning transition from home to school. The teachers know that Bryan is uncomfortable if they approach him before he is ready, so they wait to greet him until he has chosen to break free of his mother.

Kako Horiuchi, Bryan's mom, hangs her purse and coat on the parent coatrack by the door and moves with Bryan to the book corner for their morning ritual of reading a book together. This tradition is important and comforting to Bryan, for it gives him an opportunity to make the daily adjustment to the center in a calm and pleasant way. As usual, before Kako has even read halfway through the book, Bryan has begun to look with interest at the other children's activities; by the time she closes the book, he has moved out into the room. Today he joins Jerry, whom he idolizes, in the playhouse where Jerry and Nessa are removing "groceries" from a paper bag and stowing them on shelves.

The playhouse is an open, carpeted area behind the piano, bounded on three sides by a polished hardwood kitchen set. The shelves beneath the play sink and stove house a set of dishes, an old toaster, and some small pots and pans. Inside the wooden refrigerator is a bin filled with an assortment of play foods. Washable fantasy hats and dress-up costumes hang neatly from a row of blunt wooden coathooks. Doll clothes are stored in a small wooden chest for the assortment of multi-ethnic, anatomically correct dolls of both sexes that are now sleeping together in a maple doll cradle. A table and chair set are centered in the middle of the playhouse room.

Each morning Juanita or Louise sets the "dining table" in a new way, for example, for a tea party with a vase of real flowers, or with a cutting board, a wooden "knife," and a set of segmented wooden "vegetables," held together with VELCRO®, for "cutting." Today Louise has surprised the children by letting

them discover a paper bag filled with "groceries" that she has
quietly left sitting in the middle of the dining room table. The
groceries consist of some empty cereal boxes, milk cartons,
laundry detergent bottles, dog and cat food cans, and other
now-empty containers that Louise has been saving at home,
along with an assortment of plastic fruit that she picked up at a
garage sale.

"How did this stuff get here?" Yvette asks as she joins the group of
children who are excitedly exploring the contents of the bag.
    "We dus found it!" replies 3-year-old Nessa with a shrug.
    "Look, a Band-Aid box!" Jerry cries, tugging open the top to see
what's inside. "Darn, it's empty."
    "I know, we could make a *store*! Let's put everything on those
shelves," Yvette cries, knocking the play iron and the feather duster off
the shelves with a sweep of her hand. "Bryan, you be the shopper,"
Yvette directs. "Get something to put your groceries in." Although
there is a child-sized shopping cart in the playhouse, Bryan runs to his
cubbie and brings back his empty backpack, because that's how his
daddy shops.
    As their imaginations take hold, the children continue to embellish
and elaborate on their game. A shoebox "cash register" is added to the
store. Nessa tears up some paper to make Band-Aids for the Band-Aid
box. Jerry gets the idea that they need to make a drug store. The drug
store becomes a hospital as the medical kits are dragged out. The
patients are dolls, then stuffed animals, and suddenly the hospital is
transformed into a "dog doctor place." Later that morning, the pet
hospital will be transformed once again into the pet food section of yet
another grocery store.

    The convolutions and elaborations of the imaginary play
    that take place across a day in the playhouse are essentially the
    product of the children's ideas and interactions. The caregivers'
    role is tacit; the environment is set up to facilitate the kind of
    purposive, self-regulated activity that engenders meaningful
    problem solving. Young children are naturally self-directive; and
    during these periods of free play, continuity between new
    learning and existing knowledge is ensured. Through uninter-
    rupted and repeated periods of play with objects and people,
    children's knowledge of the world is gradually transformed in
    accordance with their varying abilities to use their understand-
    ing to organize and give meaning to their experiences (Forman
    & Kuschner, 1983; Monighan-Nourot, Scales, Van Hoorn, &

Almy, 1987). Fantasy play, as occurs in the playhouse, is particularly attractive to children, because here they can move through a stress-free environment in which they can learn about coping with the world through experiments that are free from risk or failure (Elkind, 1981; Greenman, 1988).

The staff intervene minimally, sometimes only to quell disputes that threaten to go unresolved and thus disrupt the flow of the play. Free play periods offer the teachers important opportunities to engage in the kind of prolonged observations of the children that yield rich information about their development in all areas. Close observation helps the caregiver anticipate the appropriate moment to enter into the child's play in order to provide suggestions to expand the play in ways that are meaningful to the children and are consistent with their interests, objectives, and abilities. Second Step's teachers' extensive training in child development provides them with the background requisite to understanding how and when to join the children's play so as to extend, rather than extinguish, the learning (Almy, 1975; Forman & Kuschner, 1983; Monighan-Nourot et al., 1987).

Squiggles on the Window

The wall next to the tables is made up of large, low windows that emit a wonderful natural light into the center. Alicia takes a moment to look out onto the large play yard. Nessa joins her. As they stare quietly out at the birds flapping around the trees, their warm breath creates frost on the cold panes. Silently, first Nessa, then Alicia, begin to draw squiggles on the frosty glass. Jerry approaches and asks, "Can I make some, too?" Before they have a chance to respond, Jerry reaches over Nessa's shoulder and rubs out her squiggles with his fist. As Nessa wails in protest, Jerry looks over his shoulder to see Tom staring at him from across the room.

Tom raises his eyebrows and says quietly, "Jerry, I think Nessa is trying to tell you something. Please show her that you understand."

"Okay, I'm sorry, Nessa. I just wanted to do some too. Look, I'll make some more." He pants hard on the glass until another frosty area appears. Nessa sniffles and begins to look interested. "Go on," Jerry offers. "You could do this one."

Jerry has been part of the Second Step family long enough to understand exactly the import of Tom's brief message. He knows that Tom likes him and that he believes that Jerry wants to behave cooperatively with other children. A central theme of the Second Step curriculum is the expectation that children will behave kindly to one another. Classroom activities are structured to enhance cooperation; prosocial behaviors are modeled, encouraged, and rewarded. Caregivers respond to children's antisocial behaviors with concern, disappointment, and, most importantly, the reassurance that they are there to help the children gain self-control and find more acceptable ways of expressing their dissatisfactions and frustrations (Bredekamp, 1987; Honig, 1985; Stone, 1978; Yarrow et al., 1973).

The Toy Shelves

Jamila and Minh simultaneously notice some new manipulatives displayed on what the children refer to as the "toy shelves." At the same time, they each reach for a peg grading board (a wooden board into which colored pegs of graduated height can be inserted). After an initial struggle to control the toy, they notice that by removing all the pegs, they can take turns inserting them back in again. Since Louise purposefully displayed the toy with the pegs inserted randomly, it takes the children a while to notice that an order can be imposed on their insertion.

The "toy shelves" are the area where fine-motor manipulatives are displayed. The program has a variety of materials designed to encourage small muscle dexterity and related concept development (classification by shape, color, size, and so forth), as well as imaginative play. On any given day, the low, open shelves might contain any of the following: shape sorters, puzzles, clear plastic bins containing bead-stringing sets, pattern tiles, small toys for sorting and counting, child-sized tongs and tweezers for manipulating tiny objects, a miniature set of the Three Billy Goats Gruff, complete with bridge and troll, tabletop blocks, bristle blocks, and both small and large interlocking blocks (Legos® and Duplos®), with accessories, to accommodate the differences in 3-, 4-, and 5-year-olds' manual dexterity. All the toys are in separate containers, which makes it easy for the children to transport them to play with on the rug or at a nearby table (Harms & Clifford, 1980).

Some of these materials are available every day; others are kept in a large storage cabinet and are rotated in the same manner as the books (Harms & Clifford, 1980). The rotation and reintroduction of manipulative materials is important because children have an opportunity to see that tasks that were once difficult and frustrating have now become manageable and rewarding. When familiar materials are reintroduced after an absence of even a few weeks, the children are often surprised to find new possibilities for play, such as sorting the beads by shape or size instead of by the more salient attribute, color.

Sometimes the staff select materials for display on the "toy shelves" that share a common attribute, such as color, or materials that adhere in various ways. Today Louise has selected a number of different manipulatives that all share the property of containing members of graduated size. On the open shelves and on a table near them, Louise has arranged several different sets of nesting cups; a set of cardboard cylinders cut into graduated lengths; the peg grading board that interests Jamila and Minh; magnetic wooden families that, when standing on a metal bar, reveal their varying heights; a set of graduated measuring cups and measuring spoons; and a miniature Goldilocks and the Three Bears family, complete with big, medium, and little bowls, chairs, and beds.

Today the toys are intended to provide the children with a variety of concrete experiences with the concept of seriation, which is also the underlying theme of Tom's special project for later this morning. The learning goal is not for the children to "learn seriation" but rather to be stimulated by the materials into making comparisons, observing the relationship of one size to another, and, for those who are developmentally ready, experimenting with ordering objects by height or length.

"Look, Minh," Jamila says excitedly. "If you put the purple ones in front to the blue ones, then you get big, little, big, little," she sings as she alternately touches the taller and shorter pegs.

Minh smiles in agreement. As they stare for a moment at her arrangement of the pegs, Bradley and Malin join them at the table. "Oh, look, clackers!" Malin says with glee as she removes two of the tallest pegs and bangs them together like rhythm sticks. Bradley follows suit, and the two of them begin to march around the table clacking their sticks.

"Hey, you're wrecking my thing!" Jamila protests, reaching out to take back the pegs.

Juanita has been observing this exchange and decides it's time to intervene. She steps in front of Bradley and Malin, and their march comes to a halt. They look up at her inquiringly, clackers momentarily silenced. "Bradley and Malin, you two know where we keep the rhythm sticks, and this is not the place!" She holds out her hands, and the children reluctantly relinquish their 'instruments.'

"These pegs belong to this toy," Juanita continues as she begins to reinsert the pegs, in graduated order, back into the holes of the grading board. "Look, this is how you use them," she announces, pointing to the board. "See how they make stairsteps."

"Oh, yeah," Malin replies in a bored voice. Bradley stands quietly, looking at his feet.

"Well, would you two like me to get out another pegboard so you can play with it like Jamila and Minh?"

"No, thanks," Malin replies. She turns to follow Bradley, who is already on his way to the playhouse. As Juanita watches them leave with a puzzled look, Louise joins her.

"You know, Louise, Malin and Bradley don't seem very interested in using the manipulatives. Do you suppose they'll have problems in kindergarten?"

Louise smiles and replies, "It's a funny thing, Juanita, but very few of these children ever spontaneously play with the manipulatives in the prescribed fashion. Yes, the pegboard does make it easy to 'see' a seriated order, but not many kids are interested in ordering the pegs just for the heck of it."

"But how will they ever learn these things?" Juanita asks in a worried tone.

"They'll learn, in all manner of wonderful ways. Some kids will discover the order accidentally as they line up the pegs to knock them over like dominoes. Others will never see anything of interest in these manipulatives but will notice that daddy is bigger than mommy, who's bigger than sister, and so on. Others will notice it by playing with rocks in the street or munching on candy canes that grow smaller as they suck. The point is that these more abstract manipulatives are useful mainly to introduce the children to the artifacts of the school culture they'll be entering soon. It's important for them to be able to demonstrate their understanding of these concepts in this fashion there. But for our purposes, I think it's just as wonderful when the children let their resourcefulness guide them in finding new and really much more creative ways of using them."

"You mean like Malin and Bradley using them for rhythm sticks?"

"Sure, don't you think that was pretty inventive?"

"Yeah, I guess you're right," Juanita muses. "I shouldn't have scolded them for doing it. I—" Just then, Louise hushes her and points over to the table where Minh and Jamila, too, have abandoned the pegboard. Alicia has wandered over, carrying one of the little dolls from the dollhouse. As they watch, Alicia is singing to herself as she quietly bounces the doll up and down the pegboard "stairs."

"*That's* how they get it, Juanita," Louise whispers excitedly, "when it makes sense in the context of *their* world." Juanita smiles as they both gaze at Alicia, who is happily at play.

Louise's knowledge of child development and her corresponding ability to use materials in ways that will extend the children's understanding are a product of her extensive training in early childhood education and development. Her greatest skill, however, is her astute power of observation, which enables her to judge, with equal accuracy, when and when not to intervene in the children's play.

The level of teacher knowledge required to make judgments of this nature cannot be acquired from a few random courses in early childhood education. Developmentally appropriate practitioners are qualified through preparation in specialized college-level programs in early childhood education. For example, Juanita's program requires supervised field experience with young children and offers a coherent program of coursework that includes courses in child development, learning, curriculum design, instructional methods, effective parent communication, and teacher responsibilities for reporting and preventing child abuse and neglect (Bredekamp, 1987; California Child Care Resource and Referral Network, 1986; National Association for the Education of Young Children, 1982, 1984, 1985a).

If the teacher is to fulfill the role of trainer, as does Louise, additional training in field supervision is essential. Implementing and maintaining a developmentally appropriate program also requires ongoing professional development to keep teachers abreast of current findings and trends in the field (Almy, 1982; Bredekamp, 1987; National Association for the Education of Young Children, 1982, 1984, 1985a).

In Partnership with Parents—Sleepy Katie and Books for Jerry

Louise takes a brief coffee break while the children are busy with activity time. She calls Katie's mom, Joanna Kaminsky, to report that Katie has a low-grade fever but seems to be in good spirits, although a bit sleepy. Joanna mentions that Katie was up late the night before watching a special TV show, but woke up in a good mood. Because this information indicates to Louise that it is unlikely that Katie's malady is serious or contagious, she agrees to keep a close eye on Katie for the rest of the morning, limit her to quiet activities, and check back with Joanna at noon to see if she needs to be picked up early.

Because of Second Step's excellent adult-child ratio, caregivers are able to accommodate the needs of children who may be coming down with an illness or recuperating from one. Although the staff agree that sick children do not belong in the center, they are equally committed to supporting parents' needs to work or study as long as their child's need for individualized attention is not jeopardized and as long as the other children are not needlessly exposed to a contagious disease.

As she sips her coffee, Louise scans the shelves of the school library to find a book about starting kindergarten, to send home with Jerry to share with his mom, Annie. She selects *Will I Have a Friend?* (Cohen, 1967), a story about a little boy who worries about going to school and making friends, and *First Grade Jitters* (Quackenbush, 1982), a funny, reassuring tale about a bunny's fears that his new teacher will say "Oogley Boogley" and expect him to know things he has not learned yet.

Louise has known Jerry and his mother since they came to Second Step nearly 4 years ago, when Jerry was one of the first babies in the newly opened infant-toddler room. She has been his teacher for the past 2 years. She knows Jerry well enough to predict with assurance that he will enjoy the books. She also has confidence in Annie's ability to use the stories to open up a dialogue that will allow them to discuss and assuage his concerns about starting school.

The Second Step staff understand that they never work with a child in isolation from his or her home environment. Hence the name, Second Step, which was born of the realization that the young child's primary learning environment is always the home. This belief guides the staff in its commitment to maintain positive relations with family members (siblings as well as parents) and to encourage the ongoing exchange of information about the child.

Louise considers adding another book, but hesitates because she realizes that it's important not to bombard Jerry with a lot of information he hasn't really asked for. She decides to let Annie know that other books are available if Jerry expresses an interest in reading more about this topic. Louise resolves to add a special column in this month's parent newsletter for parents of prekindergartners, inviting them to take a look at the school's selection of books about starting elementary school.

> Louise is clearly committed to her profession. Her knowledge of children enables her to distinguish maladaptive behaviors from developmentally appropriate ones and to use this information to support and assist parents (Howes, 1987).

Circle Time—Growing Bigger

After the children have enjoyed the morning's free play for half an hour or so, they come together for morning circle time. Here the teachers introduce the day's planned activities, discuss the weather, who's absent, or any other news of interest to the children. Sometimes circle time is held in two or three smaller groups; other times, like today, the whole group comes together on the rug. Stories and music are always an integral part of each group time.

Today, Tom has set up a special flannel board display and project in keeping with this week's theme of how things grow. The idea for the project grew out of a question Bradley posed yesterday after Tom had read the children *The Carrot Seed* (Krauss, 1945). "But how did the carrot get so big?" asked Bradley, puzzling over how a tiny seed could turn into the giant carrot harvested by the boy at the end of the story. Tom's explanation that the carrot had grown did not seem to fully satisfy Bradley or some of the other kids who had become interested in Bradley's inquiry. After reassuring the children that real carrots never grow as big as the one in the story, Tom realized that the children were also having a hard time visualizing the growth that took place out of sight, underground. So he decided that more information about the stages of growth would be valuable.

> Very little direct teaching is practiced at Second Step. But once or twice a day the staff plans a special teacher-facilitated activity that is used as a vehicle for introducing or elaborating on particular learning themes. Teacher-directed experiences offer the children new problems to solve and impart information that is not always readily accessible to discovery learning (such as how to make peanut butter cookies, how Christmas is celebrated in Mexico, and how to avoid being burned by the heater) (Forman & Kuschner, 1983; Greenman, 1988).

Today, Tom chose two read-aloud books for circle time about the stages of growth. The first concerns growth in organisms with which the children are most familiar—themselves. They giggle and relate reminiscences of their own over *When You Were a Baby* (Jonas, 1982). The children grow excited when Tom announces a fieldtrip the following day to visit the babies in the infant-toddler room. To which Alicia proudly proclaims, "That's where my baby is! You could see her tomorrow!"

Next, Tom reads *The Very Hungry Caterpillar* (Carle, 1969), an old favorite of the Second Step kids, which describes how a caterpillar eats his way from a tiny creature who "popped out" of an egg into a big, beautiful butterfly. As he reads, Tom notices that some of the younger children seem to be losing interest; this is understandable when teachers present stories to a large group, because the children have fewer opportunities to interact with the reader. Tom is able to counteract this phenomenon and focus wandering attentions by periodically pausing to ask silly questions, such as, "Do you think we'll be able to grow some of these foods here in *our* garden for *our* caterpillars? I think *I'm* gonna plant some cherry pie and maybe some lollipops. How about you, Nessa?"

"*Those* don't grow!" Nessa replies with a smug look.

"Yes, they do!" Luis fantasizes. "I'm gonna plant a cookie tree!"

After the banter and laughter die down, Tom shares some flannel board cutouts that display the graduated stages of animal growth, with a gorilla growing from a cuddly baby to a lovable big guy, "just like in *Little Gorilla!*" [*Little Gorilla* (Bornstein, 1976 & 1978) is another of the children's favorite books, which Louise often reads in both Spanish and English.] Tom then introduces flannel cutouts that show the stages of plant growth, both above ground (a watermelon) and underground (a potato). Then he describes the special activity he has planned for the day, which is designed to help the children relate what they know about how children and animals grow to a consideration of how other living things, such as vegetables, also pass through stages of development.

Because his project requires a lot of individualized attention, Tom works with only three or four children at a time. Louise and Juanita supervise the remaining 12 or 13 children, who are free to play anywhere else in the room. Although participation in projects is optional at Second Step, most of the children like to give the special activities a try.

As the children join him at the table, Tom offers them their choice of one or more "growing vegetables" from among cut-out, life-sized line drawings of carrots, zucchinis, and tomatoes of varying sizes, which he has photocopied on colored paper. Depending on interest or ability, each child either makes or is given a ready-made little "book" of blank paper in which to paste their growing vegetable(s).

Tom explains, "Today we're going to make growth books to show how our paper vegetables grow from little seeds to big vegetables ready to pick and eat. In fact, next week when we plant the *real* seeds in our garden, some of you might want to think about making growth books then to show how those *real* vegetables really sprout and grow."

"On the first page of your book you might want to show what your vegetable looks like when it's a tiny seed or a small baby vegetable, then on the next pages what it looks like when it gets bigger and bigger, and then on the last page what it looks like when it's ready to be picked and eaten."

For those children who need further direction, Tom adds helpful suggestions such as, "First just try lining up your vegetables on the table the way they grow, like this kid here, from little to big." Tom points to a poster that shows a series of drawings of a child growing from a baby to a toddler to a preschooler to a school-age child. "Then, when you're sure they're in the right order, paste 'em down on the page of your book with the glue stick."

This project is highly individualized. For the youngest children, Tom suggests that they each just pick one small and one big vegetable to paste. The idea here is to encourage them to think about relative size and to use some relevant descriptive language. Thus, Tom is pleased when Nessa notices that one of her tomatoes is the "little teeny baby" and one is the "big fat mommy."

Tom encourages the more competent 4-year-olds to arrange and order their own group of three vegetables in ascending order from small seedling, to medium-sized "not yet ripe," to the large "ready to eat" life-size model. He knows from his readings in child development that most children under five succeed in constructing only fragments of a series (Piaget, 1952a). So Tom is satisfied when most of the children are at least able to identify isolated pairs as little/big. When others go on to discover the ordered progression little/bigger/biggest, he is especially pleased.

With the most skilled children, Tom extends the activity in a number of different ways, depending on individual interests and abilities. Both Jerry and Jamila want to make their own "space vegetables" instead of using the ones Tom has prepared. They are adept at making and ordering their "weird space veggies" in graduated size, from tiny purple seeds, to Jamila's giant green spotted "big guy," to Jerry's long gray "thunder banana." Tom is pleased, but not surprised, that they are each able to construct easily and correctly a series of four vegetables in ascending order.

Tom encourages all the children to individualize the project in their own unique ways. Many of the children enjoy using crayons and markers to embellish their growing vegetables with green carrot tops, brown tomato worms, or red and green ladybugs; others ask Tom to help them label the pages of their books with descriptive text of their own invention.

> Tom's training in child development enables him to create an activity that successfully integrates mathematical and scientific concepts with experiences that further fine-motor and social development. His growing expertise as an observer of young children enables him to predict the kinds of responses children at different levels of understanding are likely to make when challenged by a problem of the kind he presents today. He knows when and how to increase or decrease the complexity of the problem so as to present a moderate, but not impossible, challenge to the child's growing understanding.
>
> Tom knows that when children are allowed to redefine a teacher's objective in terms of their own interest and learning goals, their comprehension is correspondingly strengthened. So he is always pleased when the children ask to modify the projects he has designed. This kind of flexibility and belief in the critical importance of the child's active involvement in all aspects of the learning process characterize an effective early childhood teacher (Bredekamp, 1987; Elkind, 1986; Forman & Kuschner, 1983; Gottfried, 1983). Further, because the staff members have discussed Tom's project in advance, each of them is prepared to offer the children opportunities to generalize their understanding of these concepts in a variety of different contexts throughout the day (with the manipulatives on the toy shelves, ordering rocks of graduated size in the yard, and so forth).

The Art Table—Shiny Moons

While the children take turns participating in Tom's project, Yvette and Alberto are busy at the art table. Alberto, the shy-3-year-old who rarely speaks, is delighted to play with chatty Yvette, who is nearly 2 years older. They take turns drawing big and little circles on a large piece of paper. Then Yvette begins to cut out a variety of collage material from magazines and textured paper to paste into their circles. Alberto likes that idea and tries to do the same, but he has trouble with the scissors.

"Just rip it, Alberto, that's okay," suggests Yvette.

Alberto happily rips away at the various photos and designs. He notices with curiosity that some types of paper are easier to tear than others. He carefully feels along the ragged edges of the torn paper and then runs his finger along the smooth edges of the cut paper. Yvette looks up from her cutting to comment on his discovery. "Yeah, the ones you rip get fuzzy. The cut ones are sorta sharp."

Alberto accidentally crushes a picture of the ocean that he is trying to rip out of a magazine. He starts to throw it away until Yvette remarks, "That looks neat the way you smushed that up. See, it made it get wrinkles. Feel 'em." Yvette demonstrates by rubbing the paper across her palm and then along her cheek. "See, it's wrinkly, try it." Alberto imitates her actions and repeats, "Wrinkly."

Alberto smiles and wrinkles up some more paper to add to the growing collage. He then remembers seeing some silver paper strips in the drawer that were left over from an old Christmas project. He pastes some of these on each of his circles. "Shiny," he mumbles, the word suddenly popping into his head.

"Yeah, shiny . . . shiny moons . . . *shiny moons*! We're making *shiny moons*!" Yvette joyfully gives their new creation a name and proceeds to add some silver strips of her own.

Alberto's and Yvette's play demonstrates many of the advantages of multi-age grouping of preschoolers. Yvette provides Alberto with techniques and language that enhance his exploration of the properties of the paper. Her acceptance of and interest in his contributions to their play affirm his sense of worth and self-esteem. But the exchange is far from one-sided. Yvette's experience is enriched by Alberto's curiosity; she begins to attend to characteristics of the materials (e.g., their "wrinkliness") that she might otherwise have ignored. Alberto's eagerness to play with her and his grateful acceptance of her ideas make her feel good about herself and further stimulate her thinking, imagination, and creativity.

Grouping children on the basis of chronological age alone is of questionable value, especially when caregivers are trained in child development and capable of designing a program that identifies and accommodates different levels of maturity. Multi-age grouping provides opportunities for children to interact with biological, intellectual, and psychological peers who may or may not be the same age. Competition is reduced, and a more cooperative classroom environment is often the result. Continuity and stability are enhanced because the children are assured of a 2-year stay in the same setting with the same care-givers. What will change is the quality of their interactions with peers as they move from experiencing center life as "little kids" one year to "big kids" the next. Multi-age grouping benefits teachers as well, who are able to use information acquired about the children during their first year in the program to plan learning experiences for the next (Elkind 1987).

Yvette's cries of delight attract Nessa, who wanders over to see what's going on. She notices Alicia shyly watching and beckons to her with a hearty, "Come on over! You could come, too!"

"Look, you guys," Yvette calls out as the girls approach, waving her paper in the air. "We're making shiny moons."

"Ooooh, that's pretty!" Nessa exclaims, reaching out for the pic-ture. "Could I have it?"

"No, but I'll teach you guys how to make 'em, okay?" Yvette replies with an encouraging nod. The younger girls eagerly pull up chairs and await Yvette's instructions. They listen for a minute or two and then begin to work.

"Hey, Nessa, you're doing it wrong," complains Yvette when she sees that Nessa has begun to just paste the shiny paper without draw-ing circles first.

"I needa do it this way," Nessa replies with a huff. As Yvette begins to argue further, Louise strolls up to the table and puts an arm across Yvette's shoulder.

"Yvette, that's some art project you and Alberto invented! It's great that you're sharing it with Alicia and Nessa." Louise sits down in a chair and gently draws Yvette's attention away from the activity at the table. "You know, Yvette," Louise says in a soft voice, "sometimes when you teach kids stuff, they like it so much they get new ideas of their own they want to try out."

"Yeah, but I want her to do it my way," Yvette responds sullenly, shifting her gaze back to the table to find that Nessa and Alicia have now given up pasting all together and are madly scribbling with colored markers across the circles Yvette had drawn for them. "Now they're just scribble-scrabbling!" Yvette whines. "No one likes my idea anyway!" Yvette drops down onto a chair with a thud, shoulders sagging with disappointment.

"But, Yvette, look at how Alicia and Nessa are feeling!"

"Yeah, happy, and I'm not," Yvette mopes.

"But don't you see," counters Louise, "you helped them feel that way." Yvette looks up suspiciously. "Okay, tell me this," Louise continues, "why did Nessa and Alicia come over here anyway?"

"To see what we were doing." Then Yvette's face becomes animated as she begins to remember. "Yeah, and they said they liked our shiny moons. Nessa said, 'that's pretty.'"

"Yes, and when they started out, they wanted to make shiny moons just like yours. But then they started having fun using the paper and markers their own way. You know how sometimes Tom or I make up a project and then you kids change it in ways that make it special to you?"

Yvette thinks for a moment, and then her face lights up with a devilish look. "You mean like when me and Sarah put raisins in our potato pancakes at Christmas?" Yvette grins at the memory. "'Member that? We laughed so much!"

"Well, actually it was Hanukkah. But anyway you get the idea. Well, this is the same kind of thing. Look, Alicia and Nessa are having fun just like you did. Those 'scribble-scrabble' pictures are *their* 'shiny moons.' And they like them just as much as you and Alberto like your shiny moons! Just look over there!" Louise points to the wall where Alberto has proudly displayed their shiny moon picture by attaching it with clothespins to the yellow fishing net that covers the wall.

Yvette walks over to the collage and touches one of the moons with her hand. She slowly turns back to Louise with a puzzled look on her face. "But who gets to take it home," she worries, "me or Alberto?"

Louise's face breaks into a grin. She bends down to shake her head a few inches in front of Yvette's now-smiling face. "Yvette," she sighs, "you're too much!"

By diffusing the situation when and how she does, Louise helps Yvette to see that Nessa and Alicia's revisionist use of the collage materials does not indicate a rejection of Yvette's ideas, but is as much an affirmation as are Alberto's attempts to imitate her. Without Louise's intervention, it is likely that the girls' dispute would have remained unresolved because it was founded on Yvette's defensive reaction to what she mistakenly perceived as a personal insult. Louise accepts Yvette's misperception as a perfectly understandable reaction. She comforts Yvette's hurt feelings and helps her to both reestablish her self-esteem and recapture her positive feelings toward her young friends (Bredekamp, 1987; Honig, 1985; Miller, 1984; Rogers & Ross, 1986; Stone, 1978).

As Tom hangs up the last of the "growing vegetable" books on the fishing net, Louise joins him and asks, "So what's the story with Anthony? He just wasn't interested in making one today, huh?"

"I really thought he'd like this project," Tom answers thoughtfully. "Anthony's been avoiding a lot of things lately. We should talk about him at staff meeting tomorrow night, don't you think?"

"Yeah, I think that's a good idea. I had a chat with his mom the other day and she's been concerned about him, too. She said she thought that he was worrying about her being pregnant, but there could be other things going on, too. Let's definitely compare notes at the meeting."

Tom frowns as he scans the room and locates Anthony lying on his back in the book corner, idly kicking his feet against the bottom of the bookcase. "You know, I feel sort of bad because he did do some really wonderful building in the block corner the other day with Minh, but I was so distracted with helping the kids clean out the bunny cages that I really blew the chance to give him some good strokes."

"Well, unfortunately you can't notice everything," Louise reassures Tom. "But you're right, we probably should be paying some special attention to Anthony's efforts and achievements as well as to his moping around."

Even the best of teachers are often puzzled by children's behaviors and are sometimes prevented by fatigue, doubt, momentary inattention, conflicting priorities, or personal considerations from always acting on the basis of their best judgments. Not all problems are easy to solve; many are insolvable, at least in the context of child care. Given that the state of the art and science of education is still far from complete, it is not surprising that not all teacher efforts succeed. However, Second Step's excellent adult-child ratio and paid prep time do allow teachers the time to devote to addressing these concerns, in collaboration with their colleagues and with parents.

The Block Corner

Later that morning Jerry and some of his friends are building a town in the block corner, a large carpeted area with a generous supply of smooth hardwood unit blocks of various shapes and sizes. "Here, this is the school over here," says Nessa, pointing to a tumble of blocks at the side.

"Ooh," say Jerry and his buddy Jamila simultaneously, "let's make the kindergarten room!" As they begin to construct a large rectangular area, Jamila asks, "Which blocks do you think we should use for the desks?"

"They don't have desks in kindergarten!" shouts Jerry.

"Do, too," insists Jamila. As the argument progresses, Louise sits down on the floor with the kids and calls Luis over to join them.

"Luis, your mom told me you visited the kindergarten at Vendola School when you went there to pick up your brother. Tell us what it was like."

Jamila and Jerry listen intently as Luis describes the learning centers, community tables, and big rug area that make up their new kindergarten room. "And each kid gets their own cubbie to put their papers and coats and lunch boxes in like here," continues Luis. "But my best was the yard. There's this big climber with like a fort at the top."

"Hey," interrupts Jerry, "we could make one of those, and let's make cubbies, too, for our kindergarten room!"

"I know," says Luis, "could we use those boxes from the markers that you opened this morning, Louise?"

"Sure," replies Louise, "why don't you take them over to the do-it-yourself table, where you can fix them up to look just like the cubbies Luis described?"

"Hooray," shout Luis, Jerry, and Jamila as they dash over to the table to measure, cut, tape, and color their miniature kindergarten cubbies.

Meanwhile, back in the block corner, Nessa and some of the other 3-year-olds begin to lose interest in building the model town. Tom notices that Alicia is hungrily watching the others play. "Nessa," asks Tom, "how do you think the kids will get to their kindergarten every day?"

"On a bus," replies Nessa.

"Well, gee, maybe Alicia could come over and be the bus driver for this school," Tom suggests. "Would you like to be the bus driver, Alicia?" Alicia hesitates, so Tom asks Nessa if she could show Alicia how the children use the chairs and big blocks to make cars and buses.

"Here, Alicia," Nessa directs, "you sit in this chair to be driver and we'll put these chairs behind to be the kids in the bus." Alicia sits in the "driver's seat," but still hesitates to get involved in the game.

"What should our bus driver do now?" Tom asks the group in general.

Luis runs up and suggests, "Blow your horn, Alicia, tell those other cars to get out of the way!"

"Beep, beep," whispers Alicia with a shy smile.

Louise and Tom, reflecting Second Step's educational policy, are careful to intervene in the children's play only under certain conditions. Teachers will sometimes introduce themselves into the play in order to encourage establishment or elaboration of a shared play theme; to offer relevant language ("those kind of trucks are called 'bulldozers'"); to model interactive strategies when communication among the children seems to be breaking down; or to give or get information, especially when that information serves to reduce conflict—as it does above when the children learn that Luis has actually visited a real kindergarten classroom (Clarke-Stewart, 1987a, Goelman & Pence, 1987; McCartney, 1984; Monighan-Nourot et al., 1987). In this instance, Tom provides the younger children with information relevant to both their cognitive development (how to represent a bus with blocks) and social development (how to initiate and sustain a role-playing situation with peers).

Jerry and Jamila return to the block area with their newly built cubbies. Jerry's face breaks into a grin as he gets another idea. "I know what! We need some name tags for our cubbies like the ones here at this school!"

"Yeah," answers Jamila, "and also we need a sign for the door of our classroom. But how do you spell *kindergarten?*"

Jerry runs back to the do-it-yourself table and returns with paper and pencils. He sits down on the floor and begins to carefully sound out each letter as he writes. "I think it goes *K, A, G, R, N*," he concludes. He holds the paper up for Jamila's approval. "Let's write it on our sign and see if Louise can read it."

As Jerry and Jamila work on their signs, Alicia and Nessa wander over to see what the "big kids" are up to. "What letter is that?" asks Nessa, pointing to the *K*.

"I know this one—it's a *A*," interjects Alicia. "I got a *A* in my name."

"And look, Nessa," adds Tom, "your name starts with an *N*, which makes the sound *nnn* just like in the end of the word *kindergartennnn.*"

The basic skills of reading and writing develop in contexts that are meaningful to children. At Second Step, children seek out information about how letters look, sound, or come together to form words as a result of experiences in which they see how reading and writing are useful to them. Language development and literacy are nourished through enjoyable experiences—such as participating in dramatic play or other activities that encourage communication; dictating stories of their own invention; seeing how signs, labels, and nametags are useful to readers; and experimenting, as do Jerry and Jamila, with writing their own (Bredekamp, 1987; Cazden, 1981a; Chomsky, 1981; Dyson, 1988; Fields & Hillstead, 1986; Genishi, 1988).

Clean-Up Time

Just then, Louise tinkles a bell and the class begins to sing their morning clean-up time song. As the children sing, Tom kneels down by Alicia and whispers the words of the song in her ears. "Pretty soon you'll know all the words and can sing along, too, Alicia. And now let's find something for you to clean up."

Jerry and Jamila busily begin to take apart the "bus" and return the blocks to the appropriate shelves, each of which is labeled with a drawing and name of the particular shape it is to contain. "Oops," Jamila chides herself, "silly me, I put the triangles in the rectangle department!" They share a giggle as Tom approaches with Alicia.

"Since Alicia was our bus driver this morning, I thought she might want to help you two put away the blocks you all used to build the bus," suggests Tom as Alicia waits patiently, holding Tom's hand.

"We just finished those," Jerry replies, "but I guess she could help put away the school blocks."

"Except for the kindergarten room ones," Jamila pipes in, "we want to save those cause we haven't finished making all the signs yet!"

"Oh, yeah," Jerry agrees, "I'll get the hoop." Jerry takes down a bright orange hoop that hangs on the wall above the block area. He places it so that it surrounds the part of the block school that he and Jamila want to save.

"See, Alicia," Tom explains, "this way other kids will know not to use the blocks in the hoop today because someone is saving them to play with later."

David Kuschner (1989) suggests that teachers need to be aware of the differences in the ways that they may respond to children's play, depending on the nature of the materials used. He makes a distinction between expendable materials (crayons, paint, paper)—"materials that result in a product the child can possess," and nonexpendable materials (blocks, toys, books)—

"materials that belong to the classroom and need to be used again by other children" (p. 52). The traditional early childhood curriculum is often designed in such a way that children gain an important sense of ownership ("I made it") and permanency ("I get to take it home") when they create with expendable materials, a sense that is not forthcoming with creations made from nonexpendables, where the focus is usually on returning the materials to the shelves so that other children can have a chance to play with them. The hoop is one of the ways in which Second Step's teachers acknowledge the value of attaching a sense of ownership ("We made it") and permanency ("We're not cleaning it up right now, 'cause we're gonna do more on it later") to all forms of children's play.

The center staff recognize the importance of maintaining a consistent daily schedule in order to promote the sense of security and control over their world that children feel when their environment is ordered and predictable. At the same time, the teachers are aware that the routine must be flexible enough to allow for the expression of individual needs or interests. Devices like the hoop allow *individual* children to expand and continue their special play without disrupting the daily schedule, which in turns supports the needs of the *group*. Good early childhood programs are sensitive, in terms of both structure and process, to the development of the child as an individual *and* as a member of the group (Bredekamp, 1987; Greenman, 1988).

The teachers continue to circulate around the room, calling out for volunteers whenever some out-of-place items are discovered. Louise makes sure that everyone makes a contribution. "Bradley, what area did you choose to clean up today? None yet? Well, maybe you'd like to help Malin straighten up the grocery store shelves in the playhouse. That will make it easier for everybody to shop later. Jerry and Jamila, I'm glad you were able to find the tops for all the markers you were using for your signs. Daniel, Bryan, and Yvette, when you're through putting away the Legos, you can go on out to the yard. Great clean-up job today! Oh, Katie, thanks for remembering to fill up the bunny's water bottle; I bet she was getting pretty thirsty! Latosha, maybe you can show Alicia what shelf the sorting boxes are kept on and then you can head on outside."

Tom waits by the door to escort outside the first group of children who have finished their clean-up jobs. The teachers have found that the sometimes difficult transition from inside to outside is made easier when the children move in small supervised groups.

The staff are careful to provide a variety of opportunities for the children to develop self-help skills such as dressing, eating, washing hands, picking up toys, and so forth. Allowing children to participate in these routine tasks does take more caregiver time and is often messy, but the staff recognize that children's accomplishments here are central to their healthy development (Bredekamp, 1987).

The center environment is designed so that the children can clean up with minimal assistance (Greenman, 1988). At the same time, the staff recognize that the younger children especially cannot be expected to finish each and every task—the important point is that the children are provided the opportunity to gain control over their environment by experiencing the actions of taking apart and putting back together, thus supporting the development of logical concepts such as reversibility (Forman & Kuschner, 1983; Piaget, 1952a). When clean-up time is understood in these terms, it becomes clear that the activity has a cognitive, as well as a social, function. However, when this activity is taken out of the child's control by the teachers' insistence that it be completed on their terms, not the child's, then an enjoyable, intellectually stimulating task becomes a burdensome chore.

As clean-up time ends, Sarah and her mom, Lin Chen, enter the room. Lin looks tired and apologetic. "I am so sorry we're late again today, Louise, I just can't get used to these new work hours!"

"I bet—noon to 8:00 is a big change from 9:00 to 5:00. I just wish there were some way we could help make it go smoother for you," Louise responds sympathetically.

"Well, I really appreciated your letting me know that Latosha's mom might be available to babysit. Janet agreed to pick Sarah up every evening, feed her dinner, and keep her until I get off work. Now if I could just find somebody for the weekends!"

"You look kind of tired; are you sure you're up to participating this morning?" Louise asks kindly.

"Sure," Lin responds, "I'm glad to. It gives me a chance to spend some time with Sarah! And, listen, I promise to try to get her here earlier tomorrow. I know she misses out on a lot when she comes so late."

As accommodating as Second Step tries to be to meet parent needs, the program is unable to adequately serve parents who work a nonstandard shift.

Before any more children go outside, Juanita announces that she and Lin will be walking a group of children to the local library. "Let's see, it looks like Bradley, Daniel, Katie, Malin, Sarah, and Luis are scheduled to go today."

Luis raises his hand to ask, "Juanita, my daddy and I already went to the library this weekend. Could I go next week instead?"

"Me, too, please, Juanita!" Katie chimes in. "Louise says I 'sposed to have a quiet day 'cause I got tired from watching a show. I wanna stay here and plant stuff with Louise," she explains.

"Well, those both sound like pretty good reasons; is there anyone else who'd like to go instead?" asks Juanita. "Minh, how about you? Would you like to take a walk with us?" she asks, illustrating her question with walking motions.

"Sandbox," he answers in a quiet voice.

Before Juanita has time to respond, Alberto begins to frantically wave his hand. "Yes, what is it, Alberto? I see your hand," Juanita says encouragingly. She knows that this is a good opportunity for Alberto to use words, since he is clearly interested in going on the walk.

Without a moment's hesitation, Alberto cries, "I go! I go!" As an afterthought, he adds, "Please."

"Of course, Alberto," Juanita replies with a smile, "of course you can go, too!"

> The program's generous adult-child ratio, plus the use of parent volunteers, enriches the children's day in a number of ways. For one thing, it allows an important flexibility in the curriculum, which ensures an ideal balance between child choice and adult direction. For example, if only a small number of children had chosen to go to the library today, one of the two adults scheduled for the walk could have stayed at school with the dissenters. Even more importantly, additional adults make it possible for the program to offer daily walks and fieldtrips, which illuminate the world that lies beyond the confines of the children's age-segregated environment (Greenman, 1988).

Outside Time

Louise accompanies the last of her kids who straggle outside. The large, sunny yard offers lots to do. A bike path winds around several small, grass-covered hillocks that the children love to run up and down. There are several fruit trees, and flowering vines cover the fence. Two large wooden climbing structures, one with swings and the other with two slides and a sandbox, are located at either end of the yard. An easel, with fresh paints and paper, sits under a shady awning. Yvette and Bryan make a beeline for the water table, which today is set up for "baby washing," complete with warm bubbly water, baby dolls, and wash cloths.

> The shallow plastic water table is available to the children almost every day during outside time. On very cold days, the table is wheeled inside and filled with millet, cornmeal, or water. A variety of pouring, digging, and measuring toys are always available to enhance the sand or water-play fun (Harms & Clifford, 1980).

Today Tom has brought out a movable climbing structure and left it, unarranged, on the rubber mat that covers part of the leveled ground near the room. Jerry, Jamila, and Luis are immediately curious. With Tom's assistance, they begin to rearrange it into an obstacle course. Because building and climbing are two of his most favorite activities, Jerry blissfully spends the rest of outside time inventing and testing new arrangements of the climbing structure with Tom and his other like-minded friends.

Minh and Latosha discover a small puddle of water inside the sandbox, which seeped in through the sandbox cover during the previous night's rain. "Let's stir it around," cries Latosha as she reaches for a shovel, "we could make mud soup!" Minh responds with a shy smile and a look at Louise.

Louise has been watching and understands Minh's hesitance to get dirty. She had come across some information in her reading about Vietnam that explained the dangers of chemicals, parasites, and disease-producing bacteria that could be found in the soil there. She reassures Minh with a nod and a kind word, as she has daily since his arrival, that it is perfectly okay for him to play in the clean, damp sand with Latosha. As an afterthought, she tosses each of them an art smock from the easel. "Why don't you wear these so your clothes don't get too wet."

> Normally, the staff encourage the parents to send the children to the center in clothes that are rugged and that they do not mind getting soiled. But Louise knows that Minh's family must use the local laundromat to wash the few clothes they possess. She respects their situation and has alerted the other staff to help Minh stay reasonably clean at school. Louise's efforts

here demonstrate the many ways, both tacit and direct, in which the program is sensitive to the ethnic and economic diversity of the center's population (Bredekamp, 1987; Derman-Sparks & the A.B.C. Task Force, 1989; Ramsey, 1982).

Louise had promised to start a garden project a week earlier, but decided to postpone it until the weather cleared. This morning's weather report predicted several days of clear skies, so the children are eager to get going. Today Louise is joined by Alicia, Nessa, Anthony, and Katie, who tromp through the garden wearing rubber boots and big shirts to protect their clothes from the mud. The little gardeners carry child-sized hoes and shovels for digging rocks out of the moist soil. Each also totes a bucket for collecting the rocks.

Louise plans a garden project every spring that continues until all the flowers and vegetables that the children have selected, planted, tended, and observed growing are harvested. The children are free to join the project at any time; Louise is confident that all will eventually participate, since the project includes a variety of related activities designed to appeal to the children's varied interest and ability levels (Bredekamp, 1987; Forman & Kuschner, 1983; Greenman, 1988).

As Louise begins to dig, she sings, "Ol' John the Rabbit," to which the children reply, "Yes, ma'am." As the children call out the response, they put their hands above their ears and "flap" them like a rabbit's ears. The familiar song continues, "He got a mighty bad habit" ("Yes ma'am")/"Jumpin' in my garden" ("Yes ma'am")/"Stealin' all my—my what, Anthony?—spinach?" "Stealin' all my spinach" ("Yes ma'am"). The song continues, and, with each repetition, another child gets to contribute whatever fruit, vegetable, or flower comes to mind that a rabbit would enjoy (traditional song, versions can be found in Seeger, 1948).

Music is an integral part of the Second Step program. Music, song, dance, movement, and rhythm play occur across the day and across the curriculum, not just during an arbitrary music time (Harms & Clifford, 1980). The children are encouraged to break into song whenever the mood strikes them and are always assured of other voices to accompany them (McDonald, 1979). An awareness of rhythm, in all its forms, is emphasized. The children shake bells and scratch sticks in time to a favorite song, or use their bodies to match the rhythms in dance. Awareness of auditory rhythmic patterns also sensitizes children to notice and produce visual patterns of repeated shapes, colors, and lines in art (Lasky & Mukerji, 1980). The ability to recognize, reproduce, and extend patterns is a valuable problem-solving tool that can, in turn, illuminate the patterns underlying mathematical comprehension (Baratta-Lorton, 1976).

Yvette and Jamila, wearing hats from the dress-up box, decide to take a stroll through the field.

"The field" is a small hilly area that borders the school property at the back of the play yard. Now that spring has arrived, the field is covered with sourgrass and tiny wildflowers that the children have dubbed "fairy flowers." The field has never been landscaped, because the staff believe the children need to have an area in which to explore, dream, and relax that remains essentially "untouched" by adult hands or designs (Greenman, 1988). Thus, although the children in the field are easily observed from the play yard, adults rarely join them there, except by invitation or necessity.

Getting up onto the field requires a bit of a climb up the steep, but safe, incline that rises above the edge of the yard. Because of this, the field has also become a special place for the older kids, whose climbing skills are more developed. The 3-year-olds delight in continuing to challenge one another to "make the hill." The teachers are careful to help the little ones deal with any frustration by reminding them that they too will be able to make the climb when their "bodies have grown some more and gotten a little bit stronger" (Bredekamp, 1987).

As far back as Louise can remember, every child who wanted to has sooner or later succeeded in making it to the top, although this sometimes requires extra help from a teacher or friend (which none of the other children ever seem to notice or mind). Everyone always celebrates with cheers as each child, in turn, completes the rite of passage that gives him or her access to the field. This kind of accomplishment is especially meaningful to young children, to whom it provides concrete evidence that, through persistent efforts and developing physical abilities, a personal, self-directed goal can be achieved.

"This is gonna be my Easter hat," announces Jamila as she chews a stalk of sourgrass.

"Yeah, me too, let's play Easter, okay?" Yvette suggests. "We could find rocks and hide them and pretend they're Easter eggs. And maybe we could paint them down at the easel."

"Okay, and then we could make Easter dinner and use this sourgrass for salad!" Jamila's enthusiasm grows as she adds, "And we could use fairy flowers for mashed potatoes and then we could have pretend carrots and, uh, rock cookies!"

"I'm gonna go get some pots from the kitchen," cries Yvette as she sprints down the hill. As she races past Louise, she calls out, "You know that pink paper in the paper drawer, Louise? Could we use some for ham sandwiches?"

"Sure," Louise responds with a smile, "but remember to bring back all inside stuff you use with you when we go in for lunch, okay? Are you two having a picnic up there?"

"No, Easter dinner," Yvette replies. She pauses, her face wrinkled in thought, then asks, "Louise, do you think we could squeeze a lemon from the tree to make salad dressing?"

"That would be fine, Yvette, except no lemons have grown yet this year. See," she adds pointing to the tree's bare branches, "it does have some little green buds that will be lemons later this summer, but right now they have a lot of growing to do."

"Oooh, lemme see!" Yvette walks carefully through the muddy garden to peer up at the tree. "That's neat!" she announces to Louise with a smile and a nod, followed quickly by a frown. "Yikes, I still gotta get those pans!"

The children at Second Step feel secure and protected there. They understand that their questions will be responded to, their ideas respected and encouraged.

Washing Up—The Mysterious Object Arrives

At 11:30, Tom rounds up four or five of the children, who follow him to the room to wash up for circle time and lunch. As they enter the room, the children hang their jackets in their cubbies and then head to the bathroom to wash up. The bathroom is large and contains two child-sized toilets and three little sinks, each with its own soap squirter. Against one wall rests a long, slatted pine bench where children sit to chat with friends while waiting or a caregiver may sit while helping children remove, rearrange, or reattach clothing. The walls are painted a cheery pink, and when the sun shines through the little white curtains, the room takes on a wonderful rosy glow.

While they wash, Jamila and Luis discuss the large, colorful photographs of exotic flowers that decorate the bathroom this month. "That one's really weird," Luis comments, wrinkling up his nose. "Look at that dangly thing comin' outa the middle."

"Yeah," Jamila agrees. "But this one over here, the orange one with the green, green leaves, is *really beautiful!*" Jamila loves that word, *beautiful.* She's been using it a lot lately, just like Louise. She's also been noticing lately that there are a lot of beautiful things around.

At Second Step, even the bathroom is set up as an environment for learning, for appreciating beauty, and for feeling good about taking care of bodily needs (Feeney & Moravcik, 1987; Greenman, 1988; Harms & Clifford, 1980).

Those who need to go use the toilet, whle the others move directly to the sink to wash. Tom checks that toilets get flushed, soap is used for washing, and paper towels are tossed neatly into the wastebasket. Because the staff endeavors to see that only a reasonable number of children use the bathroom facilities at any time and because the children have discussed and practiced these hygiene routines so often, very little adult intervention is required.

As Louise brings the rest of the children in from the yard to wash up, the teaching assistant, Juanita, arrives back from the library with Lin, the parent helper, and the other five kids. Alberto and Sarah are pulling the library wagon. Daniel and Malin rush up to Louise and chirp excitedly, "Wait till you see what we got! It's a real big one today!"

Jerry, Latosha, Alicia, and Nessa run up to get a better look at the large, sheet-covered object. "No taking the cover off yet," advises Bradley as Alicia stretches out her hand, "everyone gets to see it at circle time."

"But, Bradley, tell if it's a real-like one or a scribble-scrabble one," Latosha impores.

"It's a smoggy one," Brad replies with a cryptic smile.

The mysterious object to which the children are referring is what they have come to call "the picture of the week," a print of a famous painting that the library loans along with children's books, records, and films. Choosing and looking at the painting have become popular activities and form a central part of the center's arts program. The idea here is definitely *not* the provision of an elementary lesson in cultural history; rather it is an attempt to expose the children to the myriad of interesting and *legitimate* ways in which people can express what they see or feel.

When they struggle to interpret a pointillist cat or a cubist banana, the children may discover new ways of looking at familiar objects. When they recognize the worry in the face of an old man in a Nigerian film about a lost cow, or when they respond with laughter and movement to a recording of a cheerful Brazilian bossa nova, or when they can say, "She's sad," as they listen to a story about a poor Chinese girl, the children begin to discover the universality of human emotional experience and the variety of ways it can be expressed.

Circle Time—Art, Music, and Literature

Anxious to see the painting unveiled, the children hurry in to wash up for circle time. As they finish, they each find a place in a circle on the rug. In the front of the circle, the five library kids gather to stand proudly next to this week's painting. At a signal from Tom, Daniel whisks the sheet off the painting to reveal a large, impressionist view of a city.

"This painting is called 'The Houses of Parliament, Westminster,'" begins Juanita. "Parliament is a place far away in London, England," she explains, "sort of like our courthouse downtown where the judges and mayor work. Can anyone remember the name of the painter?"

"Money!" Malin and Bradley answer in unison. "His first name is Ken, I think, but Juanita says it's okay to just tell him by his last name," Brad continues importantly. "He painted it about a hundred years ago. I think he's dead now, is he, Juanita?"

"Yes, Brad, he's dead, but isn't it wonderful that we still have his painting to show us what the city of London looked like to him then?"

> Juanita wisely judges that it is not important to correct Brad's mistakes at this time, especially because the information he does remember is essentially accurate, reflects an enthusiastic interest, and is germane to his own self-constructed understanding and appreciation of the world of painters and paintings.

"What do the rest of you think of *Monet's* painting?" Juanita continues. "Yvette?" she asks in response to Yvette's waving hand.

"I think it's kinda messy. It looks like he was trying to erase part of it. And those colors are funny, lots of grays. I like red and green better."

"Anyone else? Katie?"

Katie gets up to get a closer look. "But there is red and blue. And up here is red and yellow and orange. This part is a sun. It's just mushed next to each other."

"I see a pointy building," Jerry interrupts excitedly. "It looks sort of like looking through the rain."

"Yes," Juanita replies and turns to Brad. "Is that what you meant, Brad, when you said before the painting was 'smoggy'?"

"Yeah, it's like when its real hot and smelly outside. Stuff looks funny."

"Blurry?" Juanita offers a word.

"Yes, blurry, like my eyes are dirty."

As some of the children begin to giggle, Louise interjects, "What a lovely way of putting it, Brad, 'cause when it's rainy or smoggy or foggy outside, it *does* sort of seem like your eyes have dirt across them. You know what else this painting reminds me of is once when there was a big fire downtown. Even though it was daytime, the smoke made everything look blurry, like in Monet's painting."

The discussion about the painting continues for several more minutes. The teachers keep their comments to a minimum, carefully adding new information or language only in order to further the children's thinking about the artist's vision and technique. At one point, one of the children notices that Monet painted "in pokes," not long strokes. Several of the children are very interested in this idea and want to try it themselves. Louise makes a mental note to change the paint at the easels during naptime. She decides to provide pastel and muted colors similar to those Monet chose, instead of the traditional preschool primary and secondary colors. She also considers thickening the paint a bit to further the artistic experimentation occasioned by the "painting of the week."

This activity is but one of a variety of ways in which the program supports the development of the children's aesthetic expression and appreciation. Through experience with a wide selection of art media and exposure to the works of many artists, famous ones and friends, the children's aesthetic development is enhanced. They are learning to notice and appreciate beauty and have begun to understand that the object of doing art is not to copy an adult model or a peer's creation, but rather to express one's own images, ideas, and feelings in ways that can be experienced by others (Bredekamp, 1987; Feeney & Moravcik, 1987; Honig, 1986; Lasky & Mukerji, 1980).

Circle time continues with a brief review of the rest of the children's morning activities. Yvette and Jamila tell about their picnic. Jerry tells about their kindergarten made of blocks and proudly shows his carefully lettered *KAGrN* sign; Nessa tells about how she and her new friend, Alicia, got to write on the window today and points to the smeary fingerprints on the glass to illustrate her story. Finally, with a little help from Louise, Alberto shows his new owl and tells about his uncle's visit from Colombia.

The daily review, or "what did you do today?" time, is Tom's adaptation of an idea that he brought back from a teacher training workshop on the High/Scope curriculum (Hohmann, Banet, & Weikart, 1979). When asked to report on something special they did that day at school, the children are eager to describe and, in some cases, evaluate their own activities. The review encourages the children to pay attention to their own actions and observations and consider how they might do things differently next time, which, in turn, contributes to the development of self-awareness, self-esteem, and a sense of personal responsibility for one's actions.

The review activity is also important because it elicits recall of events that are inherently meaningful to the children. They are then motivated to find the language to articulate these experiences to their peers at school and, later, to their parents at home (Genishi, 1988). The daily review is different from show and tell, which encourages children to share events or objects from home with their friends at school. Show-and-tell, or "sharing time," is also part of the Second Step curriculum, as Alberto demonstrates.

Circle time ends with stories and music, which Juanita has asked to lead today. Tom slips away from the group to set up the lunches. Louise sits in the circle with the children. The children have shown a good deal of interest in nonsense tales and extravagant language lately, so Juanita begins by reading *Jamberry* (Degen, 1983): "Quickberry! Quackberry! Pick me a blackberry!" The children laugh and love to join in when the phrasing becomes repetitive. Juanita then reads an old favorite, the folk rhyme *Drummer Hoff* (Emberley, 1967), which many of the children know by heart. By the end of the tale, even Alicia is able to anticipate and repeat the refrain, "Drummer Hoff fired it off!" Louise is tickled to notice Alicia straining to replicate Juanita's rolled *r* in the word *fired*.

After the books, Louise moves to the piano to accompany the singing. Alicia sits by Louise on the piano bench. Today Juanita teaches the children the traditional song "Oats, Peas, Beans, and Barley Grow" (a version can be found in Hart, 1982) in honor of the new garden they are creating. She is careful to introduce the melody and enunciate and explain the lyrics as Louise has taught her. Then Juanita has the children stand in a circle and act out the words as she sings, "First the farmer plants his seeds/Stands up tall and takes his ease/Stamps his feet and claps his hands/And turns around to view the land."

Singing time ends, as it does so many mornings, with Malvina Reynolds's (1974) "Magic Penny," which has evolved into an anthem for the Second Step kids. The children sing out, "Love is something if you give it away. . .''; they love the song's warm and gentle message. Singing it has become a kind of ritual that seems to promote a sense of security and group solidarity among the children and their caregivers (Greenman, 1988).

Lunchtime—Spilt Milk and Conversation

After the music, Juanita, Louise, and Tom each sit at a different table for lunch. The children are free to sit with whomever they wish.

Jerry has had so much fun with Tom this morning that he decides to sit at Tom's table for lunch. Nessa follows Jerry and sits down next to him. Tom watches Alicia as she looks around deciding where to sit. Tom gets up and offers Alicia his hand. "Would you like to sit with us for lunch, Alicia? I know that Nessa and Jerry would both be very happy if you did." Alicia looks up into Tom's kind eyes and gives his hand a squeeze of acceptance. After Alicia is seated, with Tom on one side and Nessa on the other, Tom makes a point of reintroducing her to the other children at his table, Yvette and Jamila, who are still talking about their "Easter dinner picnic."

"Who would like to pour the milk today?" asks Tom. Every hand goes up, but Tom chooses Alicia, "because she's never had a chance to do us the honor before." As Alicia pours the milk from the small pitcher into the first glass, she doesn't spill a drop. Pleased with her success, Alicia continues to pour even after the glass is filled and looks up in horror as the milk sloshes over the sides, leaving a big puddle in the middle of the table.

"Oops, Alicia, don't worry!" soothes Tom, reaching to give her a reassuring little rub on the back. "You see, there just isn't enough room in your little glass to hold *all* the milk in this big pitcher, even though I'm sure you're all thirsty enough to each drink a pitcherful by yourself!" Turning to Alicia's new friend, Tom asks, "Jerry, will you hand Alicia the sponge so we can help her clean up this flood?" Tom gives

Alicia's shoulder a final pat and adds, "Then, Alicia, you can get on with your pouring job."

After Alicia and Jerry mop up the table, Tom encourages her to fill the rest of the glasses, giving her a gentle signal when the liquid reaches the desired level in each glass. He makes a mental note to give Alicia plenty of time at the water table today, so she can begin to experiment pouring into and out of a variety of containers, exploring the concept of conservation in the most primary, concrete way.

> Lunch is a leisurely meal. None of the children are rushed; instead, they are encouraged to relax and chat among themselves as they eat. The teachers eat their lunches with the children, too, which brings a comfortable, family-like quality to the mealtime (Harms & Clifford, 1980).

At Louise's table, Bryan and Anthony interject excited comments as Malin describes the basketball game she went to with her teenage brother this past weekend. At the same time, Daniel and Sarah munch their sandwiches and stare out the window at the sunny yard. Katie's mom, Joanna, comes in the room and follows Louise's eyes to find Katie, peacefully sleeping on her cot in the dollhouse corner.

"Oh, Joanna, I'm glad you came after all. I was going to call you back right after lunch. Katie was doing just fine right up until music time, when she suddenly announced to Tom that she wanted to lie down. She fell asleep before he could even take her temperature, although she doesn't feel too much warmer than she did this morning. Do you want to let her sleep or just take her now?"

"I think I'll just see if I can get her home without waking her," Joanna replies. "She loves to sleep in the car, anyway. I brought some work home with me that I can work on while she naps."

"Well, give us a call later and let us know how she's doing," Louise says with a sympathetic look. "I sure hope she's not coming down with something, and I know you do, too!"

Meanwhile, at Juanita's table, Minh, Alberto, and Latosha are entranced as Brad and Luis reenact last night's episode of the TV show "Alf." At Tom's table, Jerry and Jamila are discussing the merits of tuna versus bologna sandwiches, while Nessa and Yvette, at Tom's suggestion, describe the remainder of the day's scheduled activities for Alicia. As naptime approaches, Tom realizes that Alicia is becoming more quiet and withdrawn. He hopes that by describing naptime as just another pleasant event in the day, Nessa and Yvette will relieve it of some of its mystique.

The teachers rarely talk to one another while they are on the floor with the children. Because they plan the day together in advance, it is relatively easy to communicate any necessary changes or modifications with short messages or even through nonverbal signals. Whether they are supervising yard play, doing a cooking project with a small group, or mixing paint for the easel, the caregivers' focus is always on the children. There is so much to attend to, given the phenomenal development of children this age, that good teachers are reluctant to miss any opportunity to observe and interact with their young friends.

Naptime

After lunch, the children prepare for naps. When the children have washed, brushed their teeth, removed enough clothing to be comfortable for sleep, and gotten whatever sleep toy they might want, they take their places on their cots, which have been strategically arranged on the rug. Those who generally sleep the longest are segregated from those who, like Jerry and Malin, only require a short nap or rest.

Louise is careful to put Alicia's cot next to Nessa's. She sits on the rug between the girls as Juanita dims the lights and closes the curtains across the windows that face the sun. The room remains illuminated by the gentle light that comes in through the uncurtained, multipaned windows that overlook the shady part of the yard. Many of the children enjoy looking out the windows at the trees or the clouds as they drift off to sleep. Today is Anthony's day to choose the "sleepytime music or story," and he selects a tape of cheerful Spanish lullabies that all the children find soothing.

As Louise gently pats Alicia's back, she notices a tear slide down her cheek onto the little blue pillow that her mom made "specially for school." Louise whispers in Alicia's ear, "I know you miss your mommy, Alicia, but she'll come back soon; she always comes back, you know that. Now try to relax, you've had such a busy day. Close your eyes and think about all the fun things you did today. When you wake up, we'll have a snack, and then your mommy will be here, just like she said she would! You'll have so much to tell her." Alicia sighs and closes her eyes as Louise suggests. Lulled by the sweet music and Louise's reassuring voice, Alicia drifts into a quiet sleep.

At 12:45, Louise takes her lunch break. As she heads for the staff room, she hands Malin and Jerry a pile of books to look at while they rest. Because the two are sometimes tempted to talk noisily while the others are going to sleep, she has positioned their cots head to toe. Juanita clears the tables and sweeps up the lunch debris as Tom monitors the rest of the children, rubbing backs and whispering reassurances as needed.

Juanita leaves for the day at 1:00. Tom is then joined by Jane Brown, who is the director of the school and also one of the morning infant-toddler teachers. Jane brings some of her administrative work into the parent-staff room so that, through the observation windows, she can keep an eye on both the preschool room and the infant-toddler room in case any of the teachers need her while the children nap. Except for Jerry, all the children are asleep now, including Malin, who has fallen asleep with her head on one of the open books.

Jerry enjoys rest time. He likes looking at books, listening to the peaceful music, and staring up at the trees, which seem to smile down on his cot below. He knows that when Louise returns in a little while, he and whoever else is awake by then will get to play a special quiet game near the toy shelves, where no cots have been placed.

Louise relieves Tom at 1:30, who heads out for his lunch break. She motions to Jerry and to Luis, who is also awake now, to join her on the rug near the toy shelves. She silently takes down a lotto game, one of Jerry's favorites, and the boys begin to play quietly. A few minutes later, Malin awakens and tiptoes over to Louise's chair. She watches as Louise snaps green beans for afternoon snack. "Can I do some, too, Louise?" Malin whispers. Louise nods and wordlessly shows Malin how to snap the beans into sections after she has removed the ends.

After the beans are ready, Louise and Malin join Luis and Jerry on the rug next to the toy shelves. "Will you read a book, Louise?" Luis asks softly.

"Please," Jerry chimes in. "Will you read the one about the monster in the boy's closet? I like that one."

"Yeah," Malin whispers her approval. "It's scary." Louise tiptoes over to the bookshelf and retrieves the requested book. She also grabs another book by the same author that she thinks the children might also enjoy. As soon as Louise settles down on the cushioned window-seat, Jerry climbs into her lap. Malin and Luis snuggle up contentedly on either side of her warm body.

The generous adult-child ratio allows caregivers the opportunity to interact with individuals or very small groups of children throughout the day. These intimate moments allow teachers and children to get to know one another better through friendly, personal social interactions. Reading to two or three children is very different from reading to a larger group, and it is an activity that good teachers welcome. When the number of listeners is limited to two or three, the teacher can pace the reading to accommodate the children's particular interests, sensibilities, and level of understanding. Language and social exchange is facilitated as they pause to examine the illustrations together or chat about a personal memory triggered by the story (Bredekamp, 1987; Cazden, 1981b; Greenman, 1988).

At 2:00, Jackie, the afternoon teacher, arrives. She and Louise check in about the day's events and review plans for the afternoon activities. Jackie asks how Alicia has been doing and inquires about Katie's absence, which she has noted from a check of the sign-in sheet on her way in the door. Louise has just finished entering her comments on the daily activity record, "Notes on the Day," where the teachers record individualized information about each of the children for the parents and to keep for their own records. Jackie reads Louise's comments and chuckles over Louise's description of Alberto's successful first show-and-tell experience.

Jackie then gathers up Malin, Jerry, and Luis, helps them get dressed and toileted, and takes them out into the sunshine. When Tom arrives back from his break a few minutes later, he joins Jackie in the yard and they exchange information about the children. Tom then goes back inside to help Louise get the nappers up and about.

At 2:30, Louise quietly opens the curtains, which were closed during naptime. As the children rise from their cots, the younger ones are encouraged to head straight for the bathroom, while the older children fold up their own blankets and sheets. All the children are expected to put away their nap things, dress, and toilet themselves as best they can. Those who have demonstrated special skills in folding, buttoning, pulling up stubborn zippers, and so forth are encouraged to help those who are just learning these skills. The children seem to enjoy showing off a special self-help talent as much as they appreciate being helped by a friendly peer.

The encouragement of helping and other prosocial behaviors is a special goal of the Second Step program. The staff spend many hours of staff meeting time throughout the school year in planning and revising strategies for nurturing the children's helping dispositions. The teachers recognize that children's interests and abilities in assisting peers varies with temperamental and environmental, as well as developmental, factors. Thus much of their planning focuses on the isolation of specific activities and teaching techniques that work best for individual children, as well as the consideration of the relative efficacy of particular methods for encouraging prosocial behaviors among small and large groups, same-age and different-age peers (Bredekamp, 1987; Honig, 1982, 1985; Rogers & Ross, 1986).

Afternoon Exercise—The Bug-Eye Hike

After all the nappers are dressed and ready to go, Louise gathers the children on the rug to talk about a special activity she has planned for the afternoon. She waits patiently until everyone is settled and looking curiously at the assortment of objects she's brought with her to the rug.

"Today we're going on a 'bug-eye hike.' Here's how we'll do it. First of all, we're not going to walk or run or climb on our hike, we're going to crawl on our tummies! And we're not going far away; we're going to hike right in our own yard, anywhere where the ground isn't too wet."

"Are we gonna wear hiking boots?" asks Bradley in a worried voice, "'cause I don't have any."

"No, you don't need special shoes because you're mostly gonna hike on the lawn or the blacktop. But you will need two things—a hoop," Louise says, holding a plastic hoop over her head, "and a magnifying glass. Is everybody ready to do some pretending today? Because you'll need to, to get these magnifiers to work right."

Louise knows by the children's nods and interested looks that they're still listening, so she continues. "Now, when you look through these magnifiers, you're going to make believe that you've shrunk yourself down to the size of a little insect." Louise pauses to demonstrate how to hold the magnifier.

"But first, you must pick a spot where no one else is and then put down your hoop like this. Then lie down on your tummy like this and look through your magnifier at all the interesting things inside your hoop. Don't forget to pretend that you're an insect! Does anyone have any idea about what they might see?"

"Yeah, ants. There's lots of 'em over underneath the windows."

"Oh, good idea, Anthony. Anyone who's interested in looking at ants can snoop around under the window. What do you think those ants will be doing?"

"I hope they don't crawl up my pants!" Latosha cries, yanking her jeans cuffs down around her ankles.

"That would tickle," Bryan giggles.

"I'll smash 'em if they crawl on me," Anthony shouts, beginning to rise to demonstrate his technique.

Louise motions to Anthony to sit down. "Oh, boy, I can see you kids are ready to go! Okay, let's get up quietly (remember we're tiny little bugs now) and walk, or crawl—no running please—out to the yard!" Louise looks over at Tom, who nods in response to her tacit message. He turns toward the door in a slow, exaggerated crawling motion that is effective in getting the children out into the sunshine in a calm and enjoyable fashion.

The fact that circle times are generally peaceful and productive is a direct result of the careful joint planning of the Second Step staff. During the first few weeks at the beginning of each term, teachers gently model and encourage the kind of give-and-take that enables all to participate in the dialogue without anyone's monopolizing the conversation or distracting others.

One important facet of Louise's skills with young children is her ability to anticipate the children's interests and behaviors. Louise takes her cues from the children and accommodates her teaching to the children's present level of receptivity. As the group begins to get restless, she realizes it is time for her to wrap up her explanation of the bug-eye hike and just get on with it. A less skilled teacher might have just gone on with her planned speech until the children completely lost interest and then, when disinterest erupted into chaos, lost her temper trying to restore order.

When Louise senses that the transition from the room to the yard may be hectic, she signals Tom to act to diffuse the situation, which he does with his exaggerated crawl. A less resourceful teacher might have forged ahead amid the chaos, yelling ineffective warnings and punishing those who most visibly disobeyed by restricting their participation in the activity. Good teachers' plans are never rigid; they are always flexible and amenable to adjustment in order to achieve a better fit with young children's ever-changing interests and abilities (Bredekamp, 1987).

As Louise works with the first group of "bug-eye hikers," Jackie and Tom supervise the others at play. Yvette and Jamila return to the field to continue their Easter dinner picnic game. Bradley, Minh, Latosha, and Alberto ride bikes around the paths. Jerry plays catch with Jackie on the lawn.

Louise asks her hikers to lay their hoops over the most interesting ground they can find. As they look with intense interest at the "little forests" revealed with their magnifiers, Louise asks questions such as, "Okay, bugs, where do you think your neighbor, that roly-poly bug, lives at night?" or "What are your friends, those ants, carrying and wherever are they going with that stuff?" Louise wants to focus the children's attention on features of the environment they might never before have noticed. She suggests, "Look how many little rocks are hidden in the dirt. How many colors can you see on them? Are you strong enough to carry them, little bugs, or could you hide behind them?"

> The point of the microhike is to offer the children an experience that will encourage them to be "keenly interested in being as observant of nature as possible" (Cornell, 1979, p. 37). Louise's knowledge of science and child development enables her to extend the children's learning here by integrating experiences with fantasy play and perspective-taking into a nature study activity.

As the bug-eye hikers explore their miniature worlds, Tom begins to sing "Exploring We Will Go," which is his "ecologically correct" version of the traditional "A-Hunting We Will Go" (version in Hart, 1982). As Tom sings, "Exploring we will go, exploring we will go/We'll catch an ant and put him in our—." He pauses as Sarah and Luis complete the phrase with "pants," Nessa calls out "bants," and Anthony offers "shoe." More children join in as the singing continues, "And then we'll let him go!" Everyone enjoys contributing their own endings to the verses or hearing the different endings offered by their friends. And no one cares whether those offerings rhyme, or make sense, or not.

> This is an instance where singing is engaged in spontaneously, for the pure joy of it. However, Tom is also aware that the children's enthusiasm for singing has cognitive as well as emotional benefits. As much as he, too, enjoys the singing, Tom is also alert to the children's varying abilities to hear and reproduce rhymes, as evidenced in the verse endings they contributed.
>
> Singing is a particularly effective way of encouraging language development and sensitizing the ear to the similarities and differences in the sounds that make up words. This ability to "hear" the rhythms and rhymes in language is a central prerequisite to the decoding skills essential to reading. Metalinguistic awareness—the ability to focus on the form rather than the

meaning of language—is a skill that makes special cognitive demands and may play a pivotal role in learning to read. Making puns, creating chants, experimenting with sound, and using nonsense words all occur in playful contexts that seem to be particularly useful for learning to attend to language forms (Cazden, 1981a). Knowledgeable caregivers like Tom, who are familiar with research findings like these, are able to take advantage of learning opportunities throughout the day that might be invisible to teachers less well trained (Almy, 1975).

While the second group is hiking with Louise, Jackie asks for volunteers to help her put the afternoon snack together. Sarah and Bryan raise their hands and jump up and down to show Jackie their enthusiasm. Hearing the words *afternoon snack* reminds Alicia that her mommy is coming soon. She looks over at Tom, who knows exactly what Alicia is thinking.

"That's right, Alicia, you mommy will be here really soon. How would you like to help Jackie with the snack, too? I bet your mommy would think that was really neat. Maybe you could invite her to have snack with us when she gets here. Your baby sister could come too!" Smiling and nodding in agreement, Alicia walks over to take Jackie's hand.

As the snack helpers go inside with Jackie, Sarah asks, "Jackie, could we eat snack outside today, 'cause it's pretty warm by the picnic tables."

Jackie takes a critical look at the tables to check for dryness and cleanliness. "Well, we haven't used those old tables all winter, so they're pretty dirty, but they do look dry." As she speaks, Jackie, too, gets caught up in the idea. "I'll see if I can rustle up some tablecloths, and we can have ourselves a little spring picnic."

"Hooray!" Sarah shouts, then bends over to explain the import of the moment to Alicia. "We're going to eat outside today!"

Second Step's program is designed to foster autonomy by allowing the children to make choices between preferred activities and make decisions that make a difference in their experience. Jackie's acceptance of Sarah's suggestion acknowledges Sarah's ability to make a meaningful contribution to her environment. This, in turn, encourages her continued resourcefulness and confidence in her potential to make a positive impact on her world (Bredekamp, 1987; Greenman, 1988).

The children's elation over eating outside for a change illustrates how flexible caregivers acknowledge the importance of

combating the rigidity of a daily schedule by periodically allowing a happy break in the routine. Good teachers know that
"children delight when the order waivers, by chance or design"
(Greenman, 1988, p. 85).

Louise's day with the children normally ends at 3:00, but she
decides to stay outside a while longer to check in with Alicia's mother
when she arrives. She also realizes that Alicia might be distressed to see
her go before Mrs. Woodbury arrives, and Louise doesn't want to
upset Alicia after her apparently successful adjustment to the center
that day. As Jackie and her helpers return to the yard with the snack,
Alicia's mom and baby sister appear in the doorway. Louise is pleased
to see that Alicia runs to greet her mom happily and brings her out to
the yard to show off the snack that she has helped prepare.
    Louise's careful observations of Alicia's behaviors on reunion with
her mother indicate to her that Alicia's adjustment to the center is
progressing well. She joins the Woodburys and, as Alicia chats happily
with her new friends, describes Alicia's day to her mother. Louise
makes a point of describing Alicia's blossoming friendships with Jerry
and Nessa, and she urges Virginia to continue to talk about them at
home. Louise explains, "Thinking about the fun she had with Jerry and
Nessa today will give Alicia something concrete to look forward to
tomorrow."

        Louise's expertise and commitment to her profession are il-
    lustrated in this anecdote. She is comfortable staying on beyond
    the end of her shift because she is compensated for the myriad
    of duties she performs outside her assigned hours on the floor
    with the children. These responsibilities include the continuation
    of her own learning about young children. In this case, Louise's
    extensive reading about the separation process informs her in-
    teractions with and observations of Alicia (Almy, 1975).

After the Woodburys depart, Louise decides to do some reading
in the staff room because she has scheduled a parent conference with
Jamila's parents, Demetra and George Cole, for 4:00 P.M. She looks
forward to some quiet time to review the day and prepare for her
conference with the Coles.
    Louise had heard through the grapevine that the Coles were
beginning to worry about Jamila's preparation for kindergarten, but
neither parent had expressed these concerns to her. Louise decided to
send home a note to all the parents explaining the program's philoso-

phy about not including more formal academics in the curriculum. In the note, she asked parents with concerns about this policy to share them with her. The Coles were still hesitant, but when Louise agreed to schedule a conference at their usual pickup time of 4:00 and arranged for Jamila to use extended care during their conference, the Coles agreed to meet and clear the air.

As the children munch on their snacks, Tom and Jackie ask them to share what they discovered and enjoyed on their bug-eye hikes. Much laughing and joking accompanies each child's account of his or her adventures as a bug. After snack, the children return to play freely in the sunny yard until it's time to go home.

At about 3:45, the parents begin to arrive. Jackie decides to corral the six "late birds" and take them together to the other side of the play yard, away from the flurry of departing parents and friends. As they cross the grass, Jackie waves to Letitia, the extended-care infant-toddler teacher, who is moving her babies back from the toddler yard into their room. Alberto and Latosha, both recent graduates of the toddler room, run to give Letitia a hug over the low, gated fence that separates the two yards.

"How come you're here?" Jerry asks Jamila as she follows him across the grass.

"I get to be a late bird today!" Jamila chirps and does a little hop. "My mommy and daddy are having a meeting with Louise, so I get to stay and play with you guys!"

Jackie's afternoon program has been so successful that many of the other kids ask to be late birds, too. The popularity is due to Jackie's talent for providing special activities that complement, rather than duplicate, those engaged in during the regular 9:00 to 4:00 day. Jackie also paces the late afternoon to accommodate the flagging energies of children who have already spent a very long, busy day at school. She tries to create an atmosphere that is intimate, home-like, and peaceful so that, at day's end, the children can calmly and happily greet parents who are still unwinding from the stresses of their own long, busy days.

Going Home—The Early Birds

Meanwhile, back in the classroom, most of the 4:00 parents have arrived. After their children have been greeted and hugged, most parents take a look at the weekly activity board, which describes the week's learning themes and lists the corresponding activities for each day of the week. Next to the sign-out sheet, the "Notes on the Day" chart includes individualized information about each child's day. Here, Delores Brown finds a message that Anthony needs a new set of extra clothes for his cubbie because his got dirty when he fell in the mud while gardening today. She smiles as she reads that her son enjoyed the gardening activity very much and "plans to plant carrot seeds next week." Jim Brenner is delighted to read that Yvette charmed everyone today with her clear and repeated singing of "Exploring We Will Go." Tran Phuoc, Minh's dad, reads with interest a note directing him to have Minh show him the elaborate skyscraper he built with Legos today.

While Louise confers with the Coles, Tom makes himself available to the departing parents. Loretta Contreras, Malin's mom, is the first to approach. "Say, Tom, I saw from the activity board that you're going to be planting the garden next week. I have some seeds for these great Finnish potatoes. They're sort of yellow, and they make delicious mashed potatoes. Would you like me to bring some in?"

"Oh, gee, I've never heard of those. That would be great, Loretta. Maybe Daniel's mom, who's from Finland, can give us a recipe!" As they chuckle over this, Kako Horiuchi joins them.

"Hi, Loretta, how are you? Listen, Tom, have you seen Bryan's backpack? It's not in his cubbie."

"Oh, they were using it to carry groceries in the playhouse. I bet it's still over there." As Kako turns to go look for it, Tom calls out, "Oh, Kako, take a minute to check out the great store the kids made. There's even a pet food section!"

Tom grabs Nessa's mom as she and Nessa are about to walk out the door. "Elise, I just wanted to tell you what a wonderful friend Nessa was to Alicia today. She's the new little girl who just moved here from Maine. They left a little early today, but I'll introduce them to you tomorrow." Tom wants to make sure that the special friendship that seems to be blossoming between the girls, and thus Alicia's adjustment to the center, will be facilitated by their parents' interest and approval.

Several of the parents take a few moments to greet one another and make plans for their children to play together in the afternoon or on the weekend.

> Many of the parents have come to know one another well through their involvement in Second Step. They look forward to pickup time as a chance to relax briefly with friends with whom they have much of importance in common. The center

holds several family potlucks and parties throughout the year to facilitate this sense of community. These purely social events offer parents a chance to get to know one another better and to network around such issues as carpools, cooperative babysitting, encouraging children's good eating habits, and where to shop for inexpensive kids' clothes. In this way, Second Step functions as a kind of surrogate extended family for those who do not have the benefit of a close, supportive relationship with relatives (Powell, 1980).

A Parent Conference

The Coles arrive promptly at 4:00 and join Louise in the parent-staff room for their conference. George opens the conversation by expressing his concerns about Jamila's academic preparation. He suggests, "What if we bought special workbooks for the kids? You know, like the ones they sell at the supermarket? Then they could practice writing the alphabet and learn to read some easy words."

Demetra jumps in to say, "We're just so worried that Jamila seems to have no interest in learning how to read or write, and we want her to be ready to do well in school this fall." They look at Louise.

Louise smiles and reminds the Coles about the school's philosophy that children learn basic skills best through experiences with language and literacy that are meaningful and useful to them. "Jamila is actively involved in these activities all the time. She loves to listen to stories, she's always asking what this or that sign or written message says, she's a wonderful conversationalist, and she's forever acting out all her favorite characters' adventures."

"But what does acting out Peter Pan have to do with reading?" Demetra interjects. Turning to George, she wonders, "Or what was that play she and Jerry were doing over and over at our house last Saturday?"

"The Three Billy Goats Gruff." George laughs and shakes his head at the memory. "Don't you remember, they were using the table for a bridge!"

"Oh, yeah," Demetra looks back at Louise, still puzzled. "Look, I know it's great fun and all, but I just don't see the connection."

"Well," Louise responds, "it's really pretty simple. First of all, when children act out stories, we know that they've been listening hard and the story has made a deep impression on them. So for one thing, it tells us *and them* that books can and do have real meaning in their lives. But also, Jamila's acting out a story is a kind of retelling. The fact that she is able to remember the characters' names, the things they did, and in the right order, shows us how complete her comprehension is [Jensen, 1985]. And, of course, being able to extract meaning from the written word is what reading's all about now, isn't it?"

"Yeah, I guess I see what you mean . . . " Demetra's voice trails off in thought.

Louise continues, "But what I really wanted you folks to think about is how well *Jamila* is already preparing *herself* for kindergarten." She pauses as the Coles look at her with disbelief.

"Well, for instance" Louise goes on, "has she been working on 'homework' at home, like she and Jerry love to do here?"

"Oh, you mean those scribbles and letters she puts together?" Demetra laughs. "I told her that she'll have to learn to write better than that before she can do real homework."

Louise smiles and gives Demetra a gentle nudge as she says, "But, Demetra, you know, this 'homework' that Jerry and Jamila have invented is probably one of the most important links between the center and public school life that the kids could be making right now. Think about what she's really telling us. She has a pretty good notion of what elementary school work *looks* like, but she's not yet sure of the content. But she is taking it seriously, and she's obviously determined to be successful at it. What better way to get off to a good start?

"And also, Jamila's scribbles really *are* writing, primitive still, but they are concrete attempts to communicate with symbols, which is really in essence what writing is all about. Have her 'read' you one of these homework pages and I'll bet you'll be delighted with what she's come up with. 'Real' writing, with familiar letters and words, will come along soon. She's got plenty of time for that" (Cazden, 1981a; Chomsky, 1981; Fields & Hillstead, 1986).

"Well, I guess I never thought about it that way," George admits, scratching his head. "I suppose she really is working real hard at this. I imagine we should really be giving her some strokes for that." He looks over at Demetra, who responds with a nod.

Relaxed and relieved by Louise's comments, the conversation continues in a lighter vein as Louise shares some of her favorite read-aloud books with the Coles. Knowing the Coles' concern that Jamila be exposed to positive images from her black heritage, Louise suggests that the Coles take a look at the literature in Second Step's collection of children's books that feature black characters and experiences that are particularly meaningful to black Americans (Derman-Sparks & the A.B.C. Task Force, 1989). George decides to borrow *Honey, I Love* (Greenfield, 1978), a book of poems about love and everyday life narrated by a young black girl, and *Ashanti to Zulu* (Musgrove, 1977), an unusual alphabet book.

"Here's one I wish they had around when we were girls, Demetra," Louise remarks, offering *Just Us Women* (Caines, 1982) for Demetra to see. "My grandmother used to take my brother and me on trips just like this girl's aunt does in this book."

"Oh, let me see that, Louise," Demetra asks enthusiastically. "This is great! You're right, there sure weren't many black girls like us to look at in those Dick and Jane books back then!" She and Louise giggle conspiratorially.

Louise is able to address the Coles' concerns about Jamila's educational progress in a sensitive and informative manner. They respect her advice and have come to count on Louise's knowledge of child development to provide them with meaningful insights into their daughter's growing abilities and attitudes. The Coles have begun to look to Louise as a valuable resource for parenting and appreciate her efforts to involve them as active partners in Jamila's education.

The importance of effective staff-parent communication is illuminated by recent studies that offer evidence that children's development in child care (especially cognitive and language development) is directly linked to mutable variables, such as home stimulation and parental child-rearing values, as well as to family variables over which center staff can have no effect, such as family structure and socioeconomic status (e.g., Clarke-Stewart, 1987b; Phillips, Scarr, & McCartney, 1987). In fact, in one study (Kontos & Fiene, 1987), "when child care and family variables were pitted against each other in regression analyses predicting child development, the family factors were more highly predictive" than the child care variables (Clarke-Stewart, 1987a).

Late Afternoon Activities—The Igloo

It's turning chilly in the yard, but Jackie decides to keep the children out a bit longer until the others have gone home. She smiles and wraps her sweater more tightly around her as Latosha and Jamila dash by to play on the grass. The girls pause to grasp hands, sing a little song, and dance an inpromptu little jig. Jerry, Sarah, and Luis have discovered some chairs that Louise had taken outside to wash earlier in the day and left out to dry. "Let's line them up and make a bus," Sarah suggests.

"Nah, we did that already today," Luis counters.

"I know it's chilly, kids, I guess we'll go in soon. You know what we need out here," Jackie fantasizes, "is one of those shelters. You know, like they have for people while they're waiting for a bus."

"Well, maybe we could build one," suggests Sarah.

"Yeah, Jackie, could we use the big blocks in the shed? Pleeease?" Jerry, Sarah, and Luis surround Jackie and jump up and down, laughing and repeating, "Pleeease" in a sing-song voice. Alberto runs over to check out the excitement and enthusiastically begins to jump up and down, too.

"Yes, yes, *anything* to save me from listening to this 'pleeeeading'!" Jackie rolls her eyes and holds her head in both hands, shaking it from side to side in mock agony. The children squeal with delight. "You guys sound like a flock of geese!" The laughter continues as the children gather closer around Jackie and follow her to the small wooden shed that houses the trikes, wagons, sand toys, and a set of large hollow wooden blocks. The blocks are heavy and awkward for one child to manage alone. This feature is intentional, for it encourages the children to plan and build as a team.

The children begin to drag the blocks from the shed. "Let's put 'em over here, where the ground is soft," Jerry directs, motioning toward the area of the play yard that is covered with the rubber mat used to cushion gymnastic activities. Jamila and Latosha run over to see what's going on.

"We makin' somethin'!" Alberto shouts with excitement.

"Yeah," Sarah continues, "we're building a bus stop so we won't get cold."

"I think you mean a shelter," Jackie suggests.

"Yeah, I saw about shelters in that book you showed me, Jackie," Luis recalls. "You know, the one about all kinds of people's houses—grass ones and rock ones, and those ones where they glue ice cubes."

Jackie looks puzzled for a moment, then asks, "Oh, you mean igloos, like the Eskimos used to build to keep warm in when they went fishing?"

"Yeah," Luis agrees, "ill-glues, so they don't get sick from being cold."

Jackie tries not to laugh as she explains, "Those are called *igloos*, Luis," she says, carefully enunciating each syllable. "They were made from blocks of icy snow that the Eskimo people carved out themselves. I'm pretty sure it's snow and not glue that held them together, but we could look at the book and find out."

"Yeah, I want to see it, too!" Jerry declares, followed by a chorus of "me too's" from the other children.

"Okay," Jackie agrees. "Let's go get it!" The group trudges inside while Jackie hunts for the book. "Here it is!" she cries, waving the copy of *Houses and Homes* (Bowyer, 1978) in her hand. The book describes how people live in various climates around the world and shows how bricks, stone, mud, cloth, and other building materials are used. The children gather round Jackie on the rug and "study" igloos together. The children have lots of questions, and Jackie uses the book as a resource for answering them. She discovers a picture of a mountain farm in Mexico that delights Luis and fascinates his friends.

Like her colleagues at Second Step, Jackie allows the children's ideas and interests to determine their learning goals. She knows that the children will understand and remember much of what they learned today about igloos and life in cold climates because it is embedded in an experience that is meaningful to them. Because the information is relevant to the children, they are more likely to persist with their self-directed task and are motivated to learn even more (Bredekamp, 1987; Forman & Kuschner, 1983; Gottfried, 1983).

The children agree to try to build an igloo of their own and march back outside to get to work.

"I'm glad it's cold," Sarah announces, gathering her parka hood more tightly around her face. "It makes me feel like more of a Eskimo."

The children work busily and happily until they are satisfied with their igloo. They are careful to make it big enough to hold everyone, including Jackie. Periodically, one or two children run inside to bring out blankets, dishes, and other necessities from the playhouse corner to furnish their new cold-weather home. When the walls are finished, Jackie finds a picnic blanket in the storage shed and throws it over the top to make the roof. At last, the igloo is finished and just in time, because darkness is rapidly approaching. The children huddle inside, sharing blankets, eating a pretend fish dinner and giggling.

After their conference with Louise ends, the Coles stroll outside looking for Jamila. "Here we are, Daddy," Jamila calls from the doorway. "Come see our igloo we made!" The Coles peer in the darkened door and laugh in delight at the children scrunched inside. Jackie takes advantage of the opportunity for announcing, "Sorry, kids, but it's getting too cold even for us Eskimos out here. We need to move back inside. Moms and dads will be coming soon."

"Waaah," Sarah wails. "I wanna keep it. I love our igloo!"

"Well, I'll tell you what," Jackie offers. "If you people will put
away all the playhouse things you brought outside, I'll see if I can find
a tarp to cover our igloo tonight, in case it rains."

"Yippee!" Jerry shouts, "then we can play some more tomorrow!"

As Jackie throws a big plastic tarp over the igloo and tries to tuck
in the sides, the children gather armloads of the playhouse supplies
and carry them back into the room. As they hang up their coats and
hats, Jackie announces, "Everyone worked so hard to build our igloo
in that cold, cold weather, I think we deserve a special treat! How
about some hot cocoa?" The children clap their hands in delight and
troop off to the kitchen with Jackie, where they all pitch in to help
cook, serve, and clean up.

After the last chocolate mustaches have been licked off, the children gather on the rug near the toy shelves, which is where they
usually like to end their day. Sarah finds her favorite Raffi tape, puts it
into the tape recorder, and carefully adjusts the volume. At Luis's
request, Jackie takes down the Playmobil® hospital set of small plastic
people and accessories, which Luis and Jerry arrange on the table.
Alberto commandeers the ambulance. Latosha and Jerry set up the
operating room while Sarah and Luis line up the little people who are
"waiting to see the doctors."

Going Home—The Late Birds

Latosha's mom, Janet Jones, arrives to pick up Latosha and Sarah.
Jackie helps Janet gather together both girls' things and makes sure
Janet sees the note Tom left about Sarah's skinned knee. Alberto's dad,
Martin, arrives and listens with some confusion as Alberto describes
how he "helt made a illgee." Jackie explains the igloo project and
encourages Martin to discuss it further with Alberto at home.

Jackie joins Jerry and Luis, who are now moving the Playmobils
listlessly around the tabletop. She realizes that the boys are probably
feeling pretty tired from their busy afternoon and decides that a
more soothing, intimate activity would be appropriate. "Would you
two like me to read some more from the poetry book we had last
week?" Jackie asks, referring to *When We Were Very Young* (Milne,
1924).

"Oh, yeah, read the one about the boy who lost his mother," Jerry
suggests.

"I wanna hear the one about the king who wanted to eat the bread
and butter," Luis adds.

"Well, I guess we'll just have to read both of them," Jackie replies with a smile. They take the book over to the couch and settle down together.

"What's the boy's name, the one with the long name?" Jerry asks.

"James James Morrison Morrison Weatherby George Dupree," Jackie answers.

"What a big name," Jerry remarks. "show where it says that." Jackie points to the words.

Jerry stares at the page and then announces with pride, "Look, here they are again. I found where it tells his name again."

"That's right, Jerry," Jackie responds happily. "See if you can find them on this page, too." Luis leans over and joins the search.

"Here they are!" the boys call out simultaneously.

"Good reading, guys," Jackie says, giving each boy a pat on the back. "Your kindergarten teacher is gonna fall over when she sees how much you two already know about reading!" Luis and Jerry give each other a smug look as Jackie begins to read.

> This anecdote illustrates how reading skills unfold naturally as the boys become curious about identifying the written symbols that represent familiar sounds and meaning in a favorite text (Bredekamp, 1987; Cazden, 1981a).

Jerry's mom, Annie, and Luis's Aunt Olivia enter the room at the same time. As the women check the daily activity records and sign the boys out, Jackie wraps up her poetry reading to the boys' moans of protest.

"You know, there's an extra copy of *When We Were Very Young* in the parent-staff library if someone wants to check it out."

"I do!"

"I do, too!"

"You do what?" Annie asks, as she comes over to help Jerry on with his coat.

"I want to check out this book," replies Jerry, pointing to the small blue volume in Jackie's hands. "I can even read it." Annie raises her eyebrows as Jackie opens to the familiar page. Together, Jerry and Luis "read" the boy's name and show where it reappears several times in the text.

"Well, I'm impressed," Aunt Olivia announces, giving Luis a big hug. "I'll tell you what, why don't we let Jerry take the book home tonight and then we could get it tomorrow!"

"Well, okay," Luis concedes somewhat reluctantly, then turns to Jerry. "But don't forget to bring it back tomorrow!"

"I won't!" Jerry promises as he skips over to the door of the parent-staff room to wait while Jackie locates the book. Jackie offers the book, which Jerry immediately clasps to his chest. With his other hand, he steers his mom toward the back door. "Hey, let's go out through the yard. I wanna show you our igloo!"

As Jerry and his mom walk into the cool evening, Jerry continues to happily chatter on about the day. "And then Jamila and I made these weird space vegetables that kept on growing bigger and bigger . . . There's a new girl today. Her name's Alicia and she's very little. Louise said I made her feel at home . . . And I can't wait to see that igloo tomorrow. We did a really good job of building it . . . Did you know real igloos were made of the most giant ice cubes in the world? Some people even live in mud houses."

Annie looks down into her son's animated face and concludes with a contented smile, "Sounds like you had another great day!"

4
Conclusion

Clearly Jerry, Alicia, and their friends fare far better in their day at Second Step than they do at Wee Tots. To what can we attribute these differences? A major answer, of course, is money. A program like Second Step incurs a cost per child probably close to twice that of Wee Tots. The greatest portion of this cost differential is staff salaries. Second Step's strong salary and benefit package enables the program to maintain generous ratios and small group sizes and to attract and retain well-trained and committed caregivers.

Second Step's superiority as a child care program is primarily the result of the professionalism and dedication of its staff. The additional funds that the program expends on its well-designed and equipped facility and yard are well spent essentially because teachers *know how to use* high-quality space and materials to benefit the children and their families. There are many unfortunate examples of good-looking, but low-quality, programs to illustrate this point. For example, some popular franchise child care operations can maintain low fees because they depend on parents' ignorance of or disinterest in the important fact that caregivers' low wages essentially subsidize the center's pretty paint job, clean bathrooms, and slick workbooks.

STAFF WORKING CONDITIONS

Asa Hilliard (1985) argues that "the teachers of our children deserve the same quality of treatment that we expect them to offer our children. High quality child care comes from high quality people" (p. 22). The National Child Care Staffing Study (Whitebook et al., 1989) demonstrates that high-quality child care requires an environment that values adults as well as children. Their findings reveal that better-quality centers have higher wages, better adult work environments, lower staff turnover, better-educated and -trained staff, and lower adult-child ratios.

The study uncovered data about the wages earned by the nation's child care teaching staff that are particularly disturbing:

> This predominantly female work force earns an average hourly wage of $5.35. In the last decade, child care staff wages, when adjusted for inflation, have decreased more than 20%. Child care teaching staff earn less than half as much as comparably educated women and less than one-third as much as comparably educated men in the civilian labor force. (p. 4)

Several recommendations of the study are designed to improve the quality of care through improving the conditions under which caregivers are prepared and work. Two of these recommendations are directed toward public and private funding and regulatory agencies. They urge the allocation of funds to increase the salary levels of child care teachers and to improve preservice and ongoing education and training opportunities for individuals employed in child care programs.

The Child Care Action Campaign (1988), a national coalition of leaders representing the academic, government, media, business, medical, religious, and child care communities, recently published its statement of policy which calls for the establishment of a comprehensive, coordinated national child care system. The group asserts that "every sector that benefits from child care should make an investment in it" (p. 15); therefore, responsibility for funding the improvement and expansion of quality child care services must be shouldered by federal, state, and local governments as well as by employers. The Child Care Action Campaign contends that "the quality of child care is directly linked to the salaries, benefits, and general working conditions of child care providers" (p. 40). For this reason, they argue that funding priorities must be directed toward improving teachers' wages, working conditions, training opportunities, and professional status.

STAFF TRAINING AND EDUCATION

Despite the fact that several important studies have shown that teacher training and education are important predictors of quality (Berk, 1985; Ruopp et al., 1979; Whitebook et al., 1989), most state licensing agencies continue to require only minimal (less than 12 units) preservice preparation (Morgan, 1990). These standards are significantly weaker than those recommended by early childhood education leaders. For example, the National Academy of Early Childhood Programs (National Association for the Education of Young Children, 1984) recommends that early childhood teachers hold at least a Child Development Associate (CDA) credential or an associate degree in early childhood education, but preferably possess a baccalaureate degree in early childhood education or child development. The academy further recommends a career ladder in which training and experience requirements increase with the level of professional responsibility.

Teacher-licensing requirements are also in sharp contrast to the amount of education and training required for certification to teach in a public school classroom. The level of preservice education required for teaching children aged 5 and older is considerably greater than that generally required of those who teach prekindergartners (McCarthy, 1988). This is true despite the fact that early childhood educators have traditionally defined the early childhood years as spanning a continuum from birth through age 8 (Bredekamp, 1987).

McCarthy (1988) analyzed state requirements for certification of early childhood teachers in the nation's public schools, which are generally regulated by state offices of education. Because most child care programs are in the private sector, standards for child care teachers are more often set by state departments of health or social services. A small but growing number of public school programs are serving preschool-age children, and they generally require that their teachers meet more stringent education and training requirements than those imposed by state licensing codes. However, McCarthy reports that there are still "19 states in which no form of specialized certification is available for those teaching children prior to kindergarten" (p. 5).

McCarthy also found a tremendous lack of commonality regarding specific features of certification. As is the case with state licensing requirements, not only is there no agreement from state to state as to the *content* of early childhood teachers' professional preparation, there is even a lack of consensus as to the *ages* of children who are considered to be in "early childhood." She discovered that early childhood certification variously encompassed the teaching of children aged zero to 4 years, 3 to 8 years, nursery school to kindergarten, birth to third grade, kindergarten through fourth grade, and so forth.

Nevertheless, McCarthy (1988) argues that states with well-defined early childhood certification requirements, even if they do not mandate that all preschool teachers meet these qualifications, "are in a better position to provide a clearly articulated progression of training opportunities for *all* teachers, including those teaching preschool children" (p. i). She contends that state certification requirements affect the quality of early childhood education programs offered by colleges and universities:

> Weak certification standards make it difficult for early childhood faculty members to build a program of study that meets NAEYC's Guidelines. The lack of a clearly defined, comprehensive program of study makes it difficult to attract students. Yet, having such a program and getting early childhood educators assigned to teach its courses is often contingent on enrollment. Without strong state certification requirements this catch-22 situation is nearly impossible to overcome. This vulnerability leads to political weakness, which . . . is also seen in the general lack of history, tenured faculty, prestige, and authority for many early childhood programs within higher education institutions. (pp. 14–15)

The National Child Care Staffing Study (Whitebook et al., 1989) determined that the quality of child care varies from state to state as well as from center to center; states with higher-quality standards are more likely to have better-quality child care. Upgrading and standardizing state licensing and certification requirements would ensure greater equity in the quality of training and education available to the nation's early childhood educators. It is important for states to reach agreement as to nomenclature, the levels and content of professional preparation, and the scope of certification (McCarthy, 1988). It is also essential that early childhood teacher licensing and certification requirements reflect the guidelines for developmentally appropriate teacher practice that have been established by the field (Bredekamp, 1987).

THE ROLE OF LICENSING

Another obvious and important question that arises when one considers a program like Wee Tots is how it could be in full compliance with all licensing regulations imposed by the state, yet remain such a grim and unwholesome environment for young children. Patently, licensing alone does not ensure quality. Wee Tots is fictional, but it represents hundreds of licensed child care programs in the United States that are allowed to operate in inadequate and ill-equipped facilities, with constantly changing and poorly trained staff, and with unwieldy group sizes and ratios high enough to effectively eliminate the possibility of any kind of meaningful relationship developing between caregivers and children, let alone between caregivers and parents.

Many child care experts argue that licensing regulations are rarely intended to do more than insure "a floor below which children's health and safety are presumed to be jeopardized. This is a far cry from efforts to assure healthy development" (Phillips et al., 1987, pp. 54–55). In California, the state's mechanisms for improving and maintaining quality operate adequately only within the realm of care funded through the State Department of Education, which demands that recipients of its aid adhere to a range of far more stringent regulations than those imposed by licensing. Although California provides substantially more state support for child care than any other state in the nation, its publicly funded programs represent only about one-tenth of all licensed child care in the state (Grubb, 1989). Even these state-subsidized programs suffer from a dwindling lack of resources, resulting in below-average cost-of-living salary increases for staff and increasingly insufficient technical assistance from early childhood consultants (Grubb, 1989).

Privately supported programs such as Wee Tots and Second Step, which make up the vast majority of licensed center-based care in California, are monitored (and then only sporadically) by licensing agents from the Department of Social Services who are not early childhood professionals and who often believe that decisions about quality are better left to parents (Grubb, 1989). The private sector also has available a number of voluntary mechanisms for improving center quality, such as the National Academy of Early Childhood Programs' accreditation system (National Association for the Education of Young Children, 1984), although few programs have thus far taken full advantage of these opportunities (Grubb, 1989). Many private programs are excellent places for children, but here good quality comes at a price, either paid out of the pockets of dedicated caregivers who sacrifice reasonable compensation in favor of maintaining their commitment to children, or by those families who are both economically advantaged *and* willing to spend as much on their preschoolers' care as they will spend later on their adolescents' private school education.

The National Child Care Staffing Study (Whitebook et al., 1989) found that better-quality centers adhere to more stringent requirements, both voluntarily and by regulatory mandate. Good programs are more likely to have completed the National Academy of Early Childhood Programs' accreditation process; to meet 1980 Federal Interagency Day Care Requirement (FIDCR) ratio, group size, and staff training provisions; and to be located in states with higher-quality standards. This finding led to another of the study's recommendations, which urges state and federal governments to adopt standards, based on FIDCR provisions and National Academy of Early Childhood Programs' center accreditation criteria, "for adult-child ratios, staff training, education, and compensation in order to raise the floor of quality in American child care centers" (Whitebook et al., 1989, p. 17).

The Child Care Action Campaign (1988) offers similar recommendations, proposing that the federal government, in consultation with child care experts, establish minimum child care standards. State regulatory agencies would be responsible for implementing these federal standards and for adopting additional regulations that meet local needs.

THE ORIGINS OF LOW-QUALITY CARE

The National Child Care Staffing Study (Whitebook et al., 1989) rates the quality of services provided by most centers in the study as "barely adequate" (p. 4). Many experts argue that the pervasiveness of low-quality child care is not caused by the loose licensing regulations per se but rather has its roots in American society's general lack of commitment to the protection and education of its young children. Jim Greenman (1988) describes the effects of this political neglect:

> [Child care housed in] the all too ubiquitous church basement is a symptom of the lack of resources this society routinely allocates to its youngest members. Programs become used to working with minimal space, minimal adult-child ratios, minimal equipment, and so on and so on. Licensing regulations designed to be floors below which programs cannot fall, in fact, become ceilings, which set the standard for the child care industry. (p. 5)

Some see the low status of child care as a direct result of the fact that day care is strongly associated with welfare and poverty, issues of U.S. life that are particularly distasteful in today's conservative social climate (Grubb, 1989; Scarr, 1984). Others point to the low status of work with children in this society, citing the poor salaries and lack of prestige that almost inevitably accompany those occupations (Hofferth, 1989). Sandra Scarr (1984) argues that "children, especially babies and young children, are devalued by their close connection to women . . . it is the low status of women that has tainted work with children, whether done by men or women" (p. 50).

Even when child care needs are addressed in this society, little attention is accorded to the implications of the fact that so few existing programs actually meet the standards of the profession. Child care quality issues are continually sidestepped by both researchers and policymakers in the face of concerns about expanding the availability and affordability of child care (Phillips et al., 1987). This short-sightedness is complicated by the fact that many people in a position to improve the system still see the primary function of child care as intervention. They regard child care as means for inoculating poor children against the future negative effects of their impoverished lives (Zigler, 1987) or for getting their parents off welfare at minimal cost (Grubb, 1989) without ever confronting the larger social problems that underlie that poverty. When child care is supported solely as a means of intervening in the lives of economically disadvantaged families, the focus is on promoting the quantity, not the quality, of programs for young children.

Sociologist Douglas Powell (1980) argues that a new role for parents has emerged in this generation that has yet to be accommodated by social policy. He describes a new "coordinative" role for today's parents; they must be able to identify, select, and coordinate the many experts and institutions who will help them rear their children. This new role represents a dramatic departure from earlier child-rearing practices and is at odds with traditional cultural norms of the U.S. family: self-reliance, autonomy, and independence. Powell illuminates a major conflict now occurring within our society between the traditional definition of adequate family functioning as autonomous and self-sufficient and the new interdependence that is a necessary prerequisite to a successful relationship between families and child care.

Most legislators and policymakers are still reluctant to acknowledge the cultural shift described by Powell in their decision making, continuing to point to parents as the sole agents responsible for determining and monitoring the quality of child care (Grubb, 1989). A major flaw in this reasoning, of course, is that parents' ability to choose quality child care for their children is seriously limited by their ability to pay. This important issue illuminates the one significant area in which Wee Tots and Second Step seriously misrepresent reality.

QUALITY AND AFFORDABILITY

In order to demonstrate the contrast between poor- and good-quality care, Wee Tots and Second Step are populated by the same fictional children. But only rarely in the real world (and then only in those few exceptional programs that are both generously subsidized and maintain full cost slots) are children of such varied ethnic and economic backgrounds fortunate enough to be commingled in a high-quality child care center (Kagan & Newton, 1989).

Recent research studies have documented the tremendous lack of parity in child care availability and usage. Goelman and Pence (1987) assert that a significant number of children in studies of child care appear to "have a 'worst of both worlds' situation: They come from low resource families and attend low-quality family day care" (p. 101). Howes (1987) found an important association between several family and child care characteristics, evidence that makes it difficult to attribute child outcomes to either factor exclusively. Parents who enrolled their children in low quality care reported more stressful lives than those who used high quality child care. Families using high quality care were more involved in and more satisfied with the program. Howes speculates:

> Thus, child care may serve as a source of social support for the parents with children in high quality child care. In contrast, child care quality appears to be a source of additional stress for parents of children enrolled in low quality child care. (p. 86)

Interestingly, two recent studies of child care quality (Kagan & Newton, 1989; Whitebook et al., 1989) report that, in the center-based care they studied, children from low-income families were not always at a disadvantage in terms of the quality of their care. Kagan and Newton (1989), in examining licensed centers in Connecticut, found that those serving the "lowest income children seem to be delivering the highest quality services" (p. 9). They attribute this finding to the fact that so many of the low-income children studied were served by government-subsidized programs, which are subject to more stringent regulations, report greater contact with community resource and regulatory agencies, and encourage much greater parent involvement in program decision making. The problem, of course, is that government-subsidized programs have sufficient funds to serve only a small percentage of the low-income children who currently need care (Grubb, 1989). The situation does not appear to be improving: the

National Child Care Staffing Study (Whitebook et al., 1989) reports that the nation's child-care centers now receive fewer governmental funds than they did a decade ago.

The National Child Care Staffing Study (Whitebook et al., 1989) had findings similar to those of Kagan and Newton, reporting that "children from middle-income families were enrolled in centers of lower quality than were children from low- and high-income families" (p. 16). They note a link between the quality of care and differences in parental fees. Although high-income families paid the highest fees, "non-subsidized, low-income families paid somewhat higher fees than did middle-income families" (p. 16). A recent Harris poll ("FYI," 1989) indicates that those families who can least afford to pay for child care are paying as much or more than families with considerably higher incomes. The average monthly child care fees paid by low-income families ($154 for families with incomes between $7,500 and $15,000; $179 for families with incomes between $15,000 and $25,000) are strikingly similar to those paid by families with middle to higher incomes ($151 for families with incomes between $25,000 and $35,000; $174 for families with incomes between $35,000 and $50,000). Only the wealthiest families paid significantly more ($332 for families with incomes over $50,000), an amount that, of course, represents a much less significant portion of the family budget. Hofferth (1989) determined that child care costs represent a substantial portion of most, but not all, families' budgets: as high as 26 percent for low-income families, about 10 percent for middle-income families, but less than 5 percent for high-income families.

Because there is a considerable lack of equity in the percentage of family budgets expended for child care, several experts have recommended that higher fees be levied on those who can afford to pay more and increased public and private funding be made available, along with the use of sliding fee scales, to support low- and middle-income families' access to quality child care (Galinsky, 1989; Whitebook et al., 1989).

Would parents choose a program such as Wee Tots if they could choose otherwise? It is difficult to assess parent preferences for particular child care arrangements when these decisions are so often constrained by the limitations of their incomes or by the range of available options in their community (Grubb, 1989; Hofferth, 1989). Recent surveys have shown that most parents see quality, particularly the quality of the staff, as more important than affordability ("FYI," 1989; Galinsky, 1989), but not all families have the option of choosing their child's care on the basis of quality alone. However, recent research indicates that most parents would appeal to quality criteria when choosing child care if other overriding considerations did not intervene.

When they asked parents how they chose the type of child care they use, researchers found that, *when affordability is not a factor*, parents made their decisions on the basis of caregiver characteristics. Demographer Rena Cheskis-Gold (1988) reports that most parents "chose their child care because of the caregiver's style and reliability. . . . Only those parents who pay the least for child care . . . say they made their choice because of cost" (p. 47). Rebecca Wheat (1989) surveyed low-income parents who, because of fee subsidies, were able to choose their children's child care arrangements from a variety of high-quality options. Wheat found that when economic constraints are removed, the quality of the staff becomes the single major criterion of choice for most parents.

Affordability is not the only reason why families might choose to use a program like Wee Tots. Parents do not always know *what* to look for when choosing care for their children, nor do they necessarily know *how* to look. Bradbard and Endsley (1980) surveyed parents to determine how they discriminated between high- and low-quality care. They concluded that many parents are unaware of what information is relevant to choosing quality care or even if such information exists. Other researchers agree that parents often select poor-quality programs either because they do not know how to recognize a good program or else because they fail to appreciate its value (Clarke-Stewart, 1982; Hofferth, 1989; Scarr, 1984).

The quality of a particular child care setting is not always immediately obvious. Knowing what to look for and how to interpret one's observations requires professional guidance (Bradbard & Endsley, 1980; Clarke-Stewart, 1982; Scarr, 1984). Early childhood educators and researchers have made great strides in the last decade toward defining the criteria of quality care (e.g., Bredekamp, 1987; National Association for the Education of Young Children, 1984). It is important that parents be encouraged to appeal to the quality criteria established by the field when they make judgments about their children's child care (Child Care Action Campaign, 1988; Whitebook et al., 1989).

THE LIMITATIONS OF RESEARCH

Even though much research evidence suggests that higher child care standards affect children's development positively, the body of research that describes the "flip side" of the situation—that specifies the effects of *low*-quality care—is still quite small. "But until we can describe more fully the negative consequences of poor child care, this issue remains largely an abstraction, and policies that trade off quality to expand the supply of child care will persist" (Phillips, 1987, p. 123). But is it really necessary to uncover more negative evidence before issues of quality are addressed?

"Physical safety factors, for example, *may* not predict advanced child development, but it only takes one child falling down the stairs to remind us that they are an essential part of a high quality program" (Clarke-Stewart, 1987a, p. 113). Just as measurable aspects of quality are not limited only to those that happen to be associated with differences in child development, unmeasured or unmeasurable aspects of quality may be equally worth considering.

Not all aspects of quality are equally amenable to statistical measurement. Not all measurement instruments are equally sensitive to the range of features that come together in a high-quality child care program. Even if researchers are unable to show a correlation between Yvette's participation in Second Step's rich music program and her present or future level of cognitive or aesthetic development, it does not follow that Yvette's pleasure in singing is not a valuable or important experience in her young life. Judgments about child care quality must not be limited only to measuring those features of child care that can be shown to produce some future end or goal for the children.

Many times what is important is not the degree to which a center meets particular quality criteria, but how the individual children in that program *experience* those aspects of care. Research efforts may lack the sensitivity to demonstrate that Alicia's traumatic day at Wee Tots will have a lasting effect on her psyche, but that does not mean that the fear and humiliation she suffers are any less unacceptable. Centers can receive good marks when measured on a scale of regulatable factors, but still be unhappy places for children. Research cannot always capture, nor can licensing ever regulate, many of the more subtle aspects of center care, such as Louise's warmth and the sincerity of her commitment to the children, which are nevertheless strong determinants of children's experience of quality.

The point here is that research is not the only means by which judgments about child care quality can be made, nor is licensing the only means by which that quality can be ensured. There is increasing consensus among early childhood education professionals regarding the criteria that define sound early childhood practices. The National Association for the Education of Young Children (NAEYC), the nation's largest professional association representing early childhood leaders and practitioners, recently put forward its position statement on developmentally appropriate practice in early childhood programs (Bredekamp, 1987). The concept of developmentally appropriate practice emerged from the synthesis of research with the experiences, insights, and concerns of qualified practitioners. NAEYC's position statement has been endorsed and adopted by other educational leaders, such as the National Association of State Boards of Education (1988), the National Black Child Development Institute (1987), and California's School Readiness Task Force (California State Department of Education, 1988). Nevertheless, policymakers and legislators have yet to incorporate the recommendations of these early childhood education professionals into their decision making about the future of the nation's child care system.

High-quality child care provides opportunities for children's optimal development to unfold. At the very least, poor-quality child care burdens young children with needlessly unpleasant memories about their earliest educational and social experiences, memories that may influence their attitudes and abilities across the rest of their growing years. Neither parents, educators, nor researchers know how to erase these bad memories, but the situations that generate them can be improved. Currently, costs and other political considerations, not the well-being of children, shape public policies about child care. Improvements in the system will come only when these priorities are reversed. Until America's children are accorded equal access to the best that child care has to offer, the economic and cultural gaps that divide them will only widen as a result of continued disparities in the quality of their child care experiences.

Afterword

An old nursery rhyme describes a "little girl with a curl in the middle of her forehead" who, when she was good, "was very, very good" and "when she was bad, she was horrid." In describing child care from the perspective of the children, Beardsley may appear to focus on extremes. Certainly the range of child care quality that can be found in centers across America is much more varied. Nevertheless, the validity of the incidents Beardsley describes can be vouched for by any keen observer who is sensitive to the perceptions of young children, and who has invested time in the diverse kinds of centers that make up the patchwork quilt of child care in the United States.

Neither Wee Tots nor Second Step is unique or atypical. Wee Tots may seem "horrid," but unfortunately there are many centers that offer young children daily experiences that are even more distressing. Second Step may appear to be "very, very good," but an examination of child care both here and abroad reveals early childhood settings that are even more ideally suited to the needs of young children and their families.

Beardsley's detailed description of the two centers and the children's experiences they elicit take on significance as she draws on both experience and research to interpret them. She shows concretely how the number of adults available makes a difference not only in the children's safety and security but in the nature of their opportunities for learning as well. Beyond that, she reveals the subtle and specific ways the teaching of adults who have a deep understanding of the science of child development differs from the teaching of those who are not well informed.

As Beardsley suggests, the scientific knowledge available to the early childhood educator, like scientific knowledge in other fields, is dynamic and changing as new questions are raised and new evidence accumulates. Recently, for example, some child care teachers have noted that the child development information that has traditionally been derived from individual children needs to be supplemented by more detailed information about the behavior of groups of children in varying classroom settings. Teachers, often in collaboration with parents, are also beginning to recognize that they are raising questions that are researchable, but not yet addressed by either child development or educational research.

Meanwhile, anthropologists and sociolinguists have begun to observe systematically the social interactions among the children in several kinds of early childhood settings. Examples of these researchers are Schwartzman (1978) and Corsaro, Dyson, and Ervin-Tripp (Scales, Almy, Ervin-Tripp, & Nicolopolous, 1991). Their studies reveal the intricate social structures and complex learnings that are inherent in the children's play and work. These findings add a new dimension to the teacher's responsibilities. How can she or he relate most effectively to these aspects of the children's social world?

Other areas of research, involving studies of child development, child care, and early education in countries other than the United States, provide interesting comparisons and raise questions about some of the assumptions underlying current child care here. For example, a recent study of preschools in Japan, China, and the United States highlights the Japanese emphasis on "perseverance, concentration and the ability to function as a member of the group" (Tobin, Wu, & Davidson, 1989, p. 192) in contrast to the American tendency to be concerned with academics at earlier ages.

Familiarity with child care, both familial and institutional, in diverse cultures, seems increasingly essential for American early childhood educators. Like the teachers in both Wee Tots and Second Step, they encounter parents from all around the world. They need to know how closely child care is entwined in and reflecting of the family's culture and how the effects of child care are dependent on that culture. To find ways of bringing parents of differing backgrounds into effective and empowering collaboration with teachers and with other parents is a major challenge.

The problems faced by child care in the United States are not unique. Ongoing studies of preprimary education and child care in 14 countries in Europe, Asia, Africa as well as the United States indicate "discrepancies between children's needs and the resources available to meet those needs" (Katz, 1989, p. 402), but the causes differ from one country to another.

The first phase of this 14-country research project, brought into being by the International Association for the Evaluation of Educational Achievement (IEA), gathered information from families and their use of early childhood care and services for their 3½- to 4½-year-old children. A second phase of the project depends on observation and interviews to examine the quality of life of children in different settings. The children's development will also be assessed in this second phase and in a third phase at age seven (Weikart & Olmstead, 1989).

The quality of life aspect of the IEA study will provide an interesting comparison to Beardsley's account of the children in Wee Tots and Second Steps. But before the IEA study is completed Beardsley's *Good Day/Bad Day* will, one hopes, have been widely read. It offers parents needed assistance in choosing appropriate child care. Where, as is often the case, choices are limited or nonexistent, it enables parents to become better informed and more articulate in working for the improvement of child care.

Good Day/Bad Day seems especially useful for policymakers, and not only because it concretizes the quality of life the children experience. Beardsley also writes with a keen awareness of policymakers' concerns. In similar fashion, she can communicate effectively with those who, sometimes with little background in early education and care, are responsible for regulation or administration.

Finally, teachers, teachers-to-be, and teachers who teach other teachers can benefit from their analysis of the factors that contribute so positively to Second Step and so negatively to Wee Tots.

Millie Almy
University of California
Berkeley

REFERENCES

Katz, L. G. (1989). Afterword. In P. P. Olmstead & D. P. Weikart (Eds.), *How nations serve young children: Profiles of child care and education in fourteen countries*. Ypsilanti, MI: High/Scope Press.

Scales, B., Almy, M., Ervin-Tripp, S., & Nicolopolous, A. (1991). *Play and the social context of development in early care and education*. New York: Teachers College Press, Columbia University.

Schwartzman, H. B. (1978). *Transformations: The anthropology of children's play*. New York: Plenum.

Tobin, J. J., Wu, D. Y. H., & Davidson, D. H. (1989). *Preschool in three cultures: Japan, China and the United States.* New Haven: Yale University Press.

Weikart, D. P., & Olmstead, P. P. (1989). IEA preprimary project: Overview and history. In P. P. Olmstead & D. P. Weikart (Eds.), *How nations serve young children: Profiles of child care and education in fourteen countries.* Ypsilanti, MI: High/Scope Press.

References

Almy, M. (1975). *The early childhood educator at work*. New York: McGraw-Hill.

Almy, M. (1982). Day care and early childhood education. In E. Zigler & E. Gordon (Eds.), *Daycare: Scientific and social policy issues* (pp. 476–495). Boston: Auburn House.

Balaban, N. (1985). *Starting school: From separation to independence*. New York: Teachers College Press, Columbia University.

Baratta-Lorton, M. (1976). *Mathematics their way: An activity-centered mathematics program for early childhood education*. Menlo Park, CA: Addison-Wesley.

Berk, L. (1985). Relationship of educational attainment, child-oriented attitudes, job satisfaction, and career commitment to caregiver behavior toward children. *Child Care Quarterly, 14*, 103–129.

Bornstein, R. (1976; Spanish translation, 1978). *Little gorilla*. New York: Scholastic.

Bowyer, C. (1978). *Houses and homes*. London: Usborne.

Bradbard, M., & Endsley, R. (1980). The importance of educating parents to be discriminating day care consumers. In S. Kilmer (Ed.), *Advances in early education and day care* (Vol. 1) (pp. 187–201). Greenwich, CT: JAI Press.

Brazelton, T. B. (1984). Cementing family relationships through child care. In L. Dittman (Ed.), *The infants we care for* (pp. 9–20). Washington, DC: National Association for the Education of Young Children.

Bredekamp, S. (Ed.). (1987). *Developmentally appropriate practice in early childhood programs serving children from birth through age 8* (exp. ed.). Washington, DC: National Association for the Education of Young Children.

Caines, J. (1982). *Just us women*. New York: Harper & Row.

Caldwell, B. (1985). What is quality child care? In B. Caldwell & A. Hilliard, *What is quality child care?* (pp. 1–16). Washington, DC: National Association for the Education of Young Children.

Caldwell, B., & Hilliard, A. (1985). *What is quality child care?* Washington, DC: National Association for the Education of Young Children.

California Child Care Resource and Referral Network. (1986). *Making a difference: A handbook for child care providers.* San Francisco: Author.

California State Department of Education. (1988). *Here they come: Ready or not! Report of the School Readiness Task Force.* Sacramento: Author.

Carle, E. (1969). *The very hungry caterpillar.* New York: Philomel.

Cazden, C. B. (1981a). Language and learning to read. In C. B. Cazden (Ed.), *Language in early childhood education* (rev. ed.) (pp. 135–140). Washington, DC: National Association for the Education of Young Children.

Cazden, C. B. (1981b). Language development and the preschool environment. In C. B. Cazden (Ed.), *Language in early childhood education* (rev. ed.) (pp. 3–15). Washington, DC: National Association for the Education of Young Children.

Cheskis-Gold, R. (1988, February). Child care: What parents want. *American Demographics,* pp. 46–47.

Child Care Action Campaign. (1988). *Child care: The bottom line. An economic and child care policy paper.* New York: Author.

Chomsky, C. (1981). Write now, read later. In C. B. Cazden (Ed.), *Language in early childhood education* (rev. ed.) (pp. 141–149). Washington, DC: National Association for the Education of Young Children.

Clarke-Stewart, A. (1982). *Daycare.* Cambridge, MA: Harvard University Press.

Clarke-Stewart, A. (1987a). In search of consistencies in child care research. In D. A. Phillips (Ed.), *Quality in child care: What does research tell us?* (pp. 105–120). Washington, DC: National Association for the Education of Young Children.

Clarke-Stewart, A. (1987b). Predicting child development from child care forms and features: The Chicago study. In D. A. Phillips (Ed.), *Quality in child care: What does research tell us?* (pp. 21–41). Washington, DC: National Association for the Education of Young Children.

Clarke-Stewart, A., & Gruber, C. (1984). Daycare forms and features. In R. C. Ainslie (Ed.), *The child and the day care setting* (pp. 35–62). New York: Praeger.

Cohen, M. (1967). *Will I have a friend?* New York: Macmillan.

Cornell, J. B. (1979). *Sharing nature with children.* Nevada City, CA: Ananda.

Crockenberg, S. (1985, October). Toddlers' reaction to maternal anger. *Merrill-Palmer Quarterly,* p. 361.

Cummings, E. (1980). Caregiver stability and day care. *Developmental Psychology, 16,* 31–37.

Degen, B. (1983). *Jamberry.* New York: Harper & Row.

Derman-Sparks, L., & the A.B.C. Task Force. (1989). *Anti-bias curriculum: Tools for empowering young children.* Washington, DC: National Association for the Education of Young Children.

Dyson, A. H. (1988). Appreciate the drawing and dictating of young children. *Young Children, 43,* (3), 25–32.

Elkind, D. (1981). *The hurried child.* Boston, MA: Addison Wesley.

Elkind, D. (1986, May). Formal education and early childhood education: An essential difference. *Phi Delta Kappan*, pp. 631–636.

Elkind, D. (1987). Multiage grouping. *Young Children*, 43(1), 2.

Emberley, B. (1967). *Drummer Hoff*. New York: Prentice-Hall.

Feeney, S., & Moravcik, E. (1987). A thing of beauty: Aesthetic development in young children. *Young Children*, 42(6), 6–15.

Fields, M., & Hillstead, D. (1986). Reading begins with scribbling. *Principal*, 65(5), 24–27.

Forman, G., & Kuschner, D. (1983). *The child's construction of knowledge: Piaget for teaching children*. Washington, DC: National Association for the Education of Young Children.

FYI: Parents look for child care quality. (1989). *Young Children*, 44(5), 39.

Galinsky, E. (1989). Is there really a crisis in child care? If so, does anybody out there care? *Young Children*, 44(5), 2–3.

Genishi, C. (1988). Research in review. Children's language: Learning words from experience. *Young Children*, 44(1), 16–23.

Goelman, H., & Pence, A. (1987). Effects of child care, family, and individual characteristics on children's language development: The Victoria Day Care Research Project. In D. A. Phillips (Ed.), *Quality in child care: What does research tell us?* (pp. 89–104). Washington, DC: National Association for the Education of Young Children.

Goleman, D. (1985, March 5). Great altruists: Science ponders soul of goodness. *New York Times*, pp. C1–2.

Gonzalez-Mena, J. (1981). English as a second language for preschool children. In C. B. Cazden (Ed.), *Language in early childhood education* (rev. ed.) (pp. 127–140). Washington, DC: National Association for the Education of Young Children.

Gottfried, A. (1983). Research in review. Intrinsic motivation in young children. *Young Children*, 39(1), 64–73.

Greenfield, E. (1978). *Honey, I love and other love poems*. New York: Harper & Row.

Greenman, J. (1988). *Caring spaces, learning places: Children's environments that work*. Redmond, WA: Exchange Press.

Grubb, W. N. (1989). Child care and early childhood programs. In M. Kirst & J. Guthrie (Eds.), *The conditions of children in California* (pp. 63–95). Berkeley: Policy Analysis for California Education (PACE).

Harms, T., & Clifford, R. (1980). *Early childhood environment rating scale*. New York: Teachers College Press.

Hart, J. (1982). *Singing bee! A collection of favorite children's songs*. New York: Lothrop, Lee & Shepard Books.

Haskins, R. (1985). Public school aggression among children with varying day care experiences. *Child Development*, 56, 689–703.

Hilliard, A. (1985). What is quality child care? In B. Caldwell & A. Hilliard, *What is quality child care?* (pp. 17–32). Washington, DC: National Association for the Education of Young Children.

Hofferth, S. (1989). What is the demand for and supply of child care in the United States? *Young Children, 44*(5), 28–33.

Hohmann, M., Banet, B., & Weikart, D. (1979). *Young children in action: A manual for preschool educators.* Ypsilanti, MI: High/Scope.

Honig, A. S. (1982). Research in review. Prosocial development in young children. *Young Children, 37*(5), 51–62.

Honig, A. S. (1985). Research in review. Compliance, control, and discipline (Parts 1 & 2). *Young Children, 40*(2), 50–58; 40(3), 47–52.

Honig, A. S. (1986). Research in review. Stress and coping in children (Parts 1 & 2). *Young Children, 41*(4), 50–63; *41*(5), 47–59.

Howes, C. (1983). Caregiver behavior in center and family day care. *Journal of Applied Developmental Psychology, 4*, 99–107.

Howes, C. (1987). Quality indicators in infant and toddler child care: The Los Angeles study. In D. A. Phillips (Ed.), *Quality in child care: What does research tell us?* (pp. 81–88). Washington, DC: National Association for the Education of Young Children.

Jalongo, M. R. (1987). Do security blankets belong in preschool? *Young Children, 42*(3), 3–8.

Jensen, M. A. (1985). Story awareness: A critical skill for early reading. *Young Children, 41*(1), 20–24.

Jonas, A. (1982). *When you were a baby.* New York: Greenwillow.

Kagan, S., & Newton, J. (1989). For-profit and nonprofit child care: Similarities and differences. *Young Children, 45*(1), 4–10.

Kamii, C. (1985). Leading primary education toward excellence: Beyond worksheets and drill. *Young Children, 40*(6), 3–9.

Kamii, C., & DeVries, R. (1980). *Group games in early education.* Washington, DC: National Association for the Education of Young Children.

Killen, M., & Turiel, E. (1985, May). *Conflict resolutions in preschoolers' social interactions.* Paper presented at 15th annual meeting of the Jean Piaget Society, Philadelphia.

Kilmer, S. (1980, November). *The effects of infant-toddler day care: An update on the research and implications for children, programs, and policies.* Paper presented at the annual conference of the National Association for the Education of Young Children, San Francisco.

Klein, E. (1988). How is a teacher different from a mother? Young children's perceptions of the social roles of significant adults. *Theory into Practice, 27*(1), 36–43.

Klein, E., Kantor, R., & Fernie, D. (1988). What do young children know about school? *Young Children, 43*(5), 32–39.

Kontos, S., & Fiene, R. (1987). Child care quality, compliance with regulations, and children's development: The Pennsylvania study. In D. A. Phillips (Ed.), *Quality in child care: What does research tell us?* (pp. 57–79). Washington, DC: National Association for the Education of Young Children.

Krauss, R. (1945). *The carrot seed.* New York: Harper & Row.

Kuschner, D. (1989). "Put your name on your painting, but . . . the blocks go back on the shelves." *Young Children, 45*(1), 49–56.

Lasky, L., & Mukerji, R. (1980). *Art: Basic for young children.* Washington, DC: National Association for the Education of Young Children.

Logue, M. E., Eheart, B. K. & Leavitt, R. L. (1986). Staff training: What difference does it make? *Young Children, 41*(5), 8–9.

Mattick, I. (1981). The teacher's role in helping young children develop language competence. In C. B. Cazden (Ed.), *Language in early childhood education* (rev. ed.) (pp. 83–95). Washington, DC: National Association for the Education of Young Children.

McCarthy, J. (1988). *State certification of early childhood teachers: An analysis of the 50 states and the District of Columbia.* Washington, DC: National Association for the Education of Young Children.

McCartney, K. (1984). Effect of quality of day-care environment on children's language development. *Developmental Psychology, 20,* 244–260.

McCartney, K., Scarr, S., Phillips, D., Grajek, S., & Schwarz, C. (1982). Environmental differences among day care centers and their effects on children's levels of intellectual, language, and social development. In E. Zigler & E. Gordon (Eds.), *Day care: Scientific and social policy issues* (pp. 126–151). Boston: Auburn House.

McCracken, J. B. (1986). *So many goodbyes: Ways to ease the transition between home and groups for young children.* Washington, DC: National Association for the Education of Young Children.

McDonald, D. T. (1979). *Music in our lives: The early years.* Washington, DC: National Association for the Education of Young Children.

McLaughlin, R., & Wood, L. (1969). *The small singer.* Glendale, CA: Bowmar.

Miller, C. S. (1984). Building self-control: Discipline for young children. *Young Children, 40*(1), 15–19.

Milne, A. A. (1924). *When we were very young.* New York: Dutton.

Mischel, W. (1970). Sex-typing and socialization. In P. H. Mussen (Ed.), *Carmichael's manual of child psychology* (Vol. 2) (pp. 3–72). New York: Wiley.

Monighan-Nourot, P., Scales, B., Van Hoorn, J., & Almy, M. (1987). *Looking at children's play: A bridge between theory and practice.* New York: Teachers College Press.

Morgan, G. (1990). *The national state of child care regulation, 1989.* Washington, DC: National Association for the Education of Young Children.

Musgrove, M. (1977). *Ashanti to Zulu.* New York: Dial.

National Association for the Education of Young Children. (1982). *Early childhood teacher education guidelines for four- and five-year programs.* Washington, DC: Author.

National Association for the Education of Young Children. (1984). *Accreditation criteria and procedures of the National Academy of Early Childhood Programs.* Washington, DC: Author.

National Association for the Education of Young Children. (1985a). *Guidelines for early childhood education programs in associate degree granting institutions.* Washington, DC: Author.

National Association for the Education of Young Children. (1985b). *In whose hands? A demographic factsheet on child care providers.* Washington, DC: Author.

National Association of State Boards of Education. (1988). *Right from the start: The report of the NASBE task force on early childhood education.* Alexandria, VA: Author.

National Black Child Development Institute, Inc. (1987). *Safeguards: Guidelines for establishing programs for four-year-olds in the public schools.* Washington, DC: Author.

Oppenheim, J., Brenner, B., & Boegehold, B. (1986). *Choosing books for kids.* New York: Ballantine/Bank Street.

Phillips, D. A. (Ed.). (1987). *Quality in child care: What does research tell us?* Washington, DC: National Association for the Education of Young Children.

Phillips, D. A., Scarr, S., & McCartney, K. (1987). Dimensions and effects of child care quality: The Bermuda study. In D. A. Phillips (Ed.), *Quality in child care: What does research tell us?* (pp. 43–56). Washington, DC: National Association for the Education of Young Children.

Piaget, J. (1932). *The moral judgment of the child* (M. Gabain, trans.). New York: Macmillan.

Piaget, J. (1950). *The psychology of intelligence.* London: Routledge & Kegan Paul.

Piaget, J. (1952a). *The child's conception of number.* London: Routledge & Kegan Paul.

Piaget, J. (1952b). *The origins of intelligence in children.* New York: Norton.

Powell, D. R. (1980). Toward a socioecological perspective of relations between parents and child care programs. In S. Kilmer (Ed.), *Advances in early education and day care* (Vol. 1) (pp. 203–226). Greenwich, CT: JAI Press.

Quackenbush, R. (1982). *First grade jitters.* New York: Lippincott.

Ramsey, P. G. (1982). Multicultural education in early childhood. *Young Children, 37*(2), 13–24.

Reifel, S. (1988). Children's thinking about their early education experiences. *Theory into Practice, 27*(1), 62–66.

Reuter, J., & Yunik, G. (1973). Social interaction in nursery schools. *Developmental Psychology, 9,* 319–325.

Reynolds, M. (1975). *The Malvina Reynolds songbook.* Berkeley, CA: Schroder Music Co.

Richardson, D. (1985). Day care: Men need not apply. *Mother Jones, 10,* 60.

Rogers, D.L., & Ross, D. D. (1986). Encouraging positive social interaction among young children. *Young Children, 41*(3), 12–17.

Rubenstein, J., & Howes, C. (1979). Caregiving and infant behavior in day care and in homes. *Developmental Psychology 15,* 1–24.

Ruopp, R., Travers, J., Glantz, F., & Coelen, C. (1979). *Children at the center:*

Final report of the National Day Care Study. Cambridge, MA: Abt
Associates.

Scarr, S. (1984). *Mother care/other care.* New York: Basic Books.

Schwartz, P. (1983). Length of day care attendance and attachment behaviors
in eighteen month old infants. *Child Development, 54,* 1073–1078.

Schweinhart, L. J., Weikart, D. P., & Larner, M. B. (1986). Consequences of
three preschool curriculum models through age 15. *Early Childhood
Research Quarterly, 1,* 15–45.

Seeger, R. C. (1948). *American folk songs for children.* New York: Doubleday.

Segal, J., & Segal, Z. (1986, Summer). The powerful world of peer relationships. *American Educator,* pp. 14–17, 45.

Smith, P., & Connolly, K. (1981). *The behavioral ecology of the preschool.*
Cambridge, England: Cambridge University Press.

Sprung, B. (1975). Opening the options for children: A nonsexist approach to
early childhood education. *Young Children, 31*(1), 12–21.

State of California Department of Social Services. (1986). Chapter 1: Child
day care: General licensing requirements & Chapter 2: Day care centers.
In *California Administrative Code, Title 22, Division 12.*

Stoddart, T., & Turiel, E. (1985). Children's concepts of cross-gender activities. *Child Development, 56,* 1241–1252.

Stone, J. G. (1978). *A guide to discipline* (rev. ed.). Washington, DC: National
Association for the Education of Young Children.

Tizard, B. (1981). Language at home and at school. In C. B. Cazden (Ed.),
Language in early childhood education (rev. ed.) (pp. 17–27). Washington, DC: National Association for the Education of Young Children.

Tizard, B., Cooperman, O., Joseph, A., & Tizard, J. (1972). Environmental
effects on language development: A study of young children in long-stay
residential nurseries. *Child Development, 43,* 337–358.

Vandell, D., & Powers, C. (1983). Daycare quality and children's free play
activities. *American Journal of Orthopsychiatry, 53,* 293–300.

Wheat, R. (1989). *Diversity in day care: Options and issues.* Lancaster, PA:
Technomic Press.

Whitebook, M., Howes, C., Darrah, R. & Friedman, J. (1981), January-Febru-
ary). Who's minding the child care workers?: A look at staff burnout.
Children Today, pp. 2–6.

Whitebook, M., Howes, C., & Phillips, D. (1989). *Who cares? Child care
teachers and the quality of care in America. Executive summary of the
National Child Care Staffing Study.* Oakland, CA: Child Care Employee
Project.

Willer, B. (1987). Quality or affordability: Trade-offs for early childhood
programs? *Young Children, 42*(6), 41–43.

Yarrow, M. R., Scott, P. M., & Waxler, C. Z. (1973). Learning concern for
others. *Developmental Psychology, 8,* 240–260.

Zigler, E. (1987). Formal schooling for four-year-olds? No. *American Psychologist, 42*(3), 254–260.

Index

House corner, 16. *See also* Playhouse
Houses and Homes (Bowyer), 123
"Houses of Parliament, Westminster,
    The" (painting), 104
Howes, C., 2, 4, 9, 10, 11, 14, 42, 61, 62,
    63, 85, 127–128, 130, 131–132, 134,
    135, 136
Hygiene, 20, 103

Igloos, 29, 122–124
Illness
    of child care staff, 10
    of children, 32, 83–84, 108
Income. *See* Affordability; Parents,
    income of
Individual differences and needs,
    accommodating, 17, 21, 23, 24, 28,
    32, 42, 47, 48, 64, 70, 71, 73, 77, 84,
    87–88, 89, 96, 100, 109, 110, 111–112,
    113. *See also* Developmental
    differences, accommodating
Insurance, 43
Interactions, staff, 45, 88, 92, 109, 111,
    113. *See also* Parents,
    communication with
Interactions, adult-child, 20, 45, 46–47,
    71–75, 110–111. *See also* Attachment;
    Discipline; Guidance
    managerial, 14, 44, 46, 47
    verbal, 23, 46–47, 71–75, 94, 108, 111
Interactions, peer, 25, 35, 36, 37, 38, 44,
    71, 90
International Association for the
    Evaluation of Educational
    Achievement (IEA), 141
Intervention, child care as, ix, 133

Jalongo, M. R., 22, 75
Jamberry (Degen), 106
James James Morrison Morrison
    Weatherby George Dupree
    (character in poem), 125
Jensen, M. A., 120
Jonas, A., 86
Joseph, A., 47
Just Us Women (Caines), 121

Kagan, S. L., 134
Katz, L. G., 140
Kamii, C., 12, 13, 46

Kantor, R., 69
Killen, M., 36, 44
Kilmer, S., 42
Kindergarten
    preparation for, 116, 120, 125
    preschoolers' image of, 33, 34, 67, 69
    transition to, 17, 67–69, 84–85, 125
Klein, E., 69
Kontos, S., 9, 63, 121
Krauss, R., 85
Kuschner, David, 12, 13, 23, 24, 30, 33, 46,
    78, 79, 85, 88, 95–96, 97, 100, 123

Language development, 23, 46–47, 61,
    63, 66, 73–74, 89, 95, 114–115, 121
    language play, 66, 106, 114, 115
    research on, 2, 32, 46–47, 61, 63, 73
    second-language acquisition, 31–32, 60,
    70, 98
    teachers' encouragement for, 105, 106,
    111
    use of vulgarities in, 38
Larner, M. B., 62
Lasky, L., 30, 65, 101, 105
Learning. *See also* Curriculum
    child-initiated, 12, 13, 30, 32, 33, 61,
    78–79, 82, 88, 94–95, 100, 104, 113,
    123, 125
    teacher-directed, 12, 26–31, 32, 34, 35,
    36, 61, 85–88, 112–114
    research on, 12–13, 61–62
Leavitt, R. L., 62
Licensing
    and child care quality, xi, 7, 130–132,
    137
    regulations, in California, 4, 7–8, 43,
    45, 46, 51
    regulations, in other states, 4, 7–8,
    128–129
    training requirements of, 10, 128–129,
    130
Literacy, development of, 12, 13, 94–95,
    114–115, 119–120. *See also* Books in
    the early childhood curriculum
    dictated text, 13, 88, 95
    learning to read, 13, 95, 114–115,
    119–120, 125
    learning to write, 13, 34, 64, 95, 120
Little Gorilla (Bornstein), 86
Logue, M. E., 62

About the Author

Lyda Beardsley is an educational consultant, specializing in curriculum development, teacher education, and administration of early childhood programs. She has been a preschool and elementary teacher and child care administrator in San Francisco, Berkeley, and Oakland. She was a supervisor of teacher education and evaluator of teacher credential programs at the University of California, Berkeley, where she is currently completing a Ph.D. in educational psychology. In addition to her interest in quality issues in child care, she has conducted research on moral and social development and educational policy.

Date Due

BRODART, CO.   Cat. No. 23-233-003   Printed in U.S.A.